Kaleidoscope for Becoming:

A Grimoire of Revolution

By,

Celeste Emelia Mattingly, LCSW

Published by

Adam Kadmon Publishing
P.O. Box 330039
West Hartford, Connecticut 06133
USA

Kaleidoscope for Becoming: A Grimoire of Revolution

Copyright © 2025 by Celeste Emelia Mattingly, LCSW

All rights reserved. No part of this book may be used or reproduced in any manner whatsoever, including photocopying or internet use, without written permission from the author or contributor.

Properly credited or cited fair use brief quotations are allowed.

The information in this book is intended to be educational and is not intended to directly or indirectly replace any form of medical treatment or 12-Step recovery program. The author, contributors, and publisher are in no way either directly or indirectly liable or responsible for any use or misuse of this material.

Printed in the United States of America.
Includes illustrations, bibliographical references, glossary, and index.
ISBN: 978-0-9859819-4-5
https://celestialempowerment.com

Celestial Psychology® is a registered trademark of Celeste E. Mattingly, LCSW.
US Patent and Trademark Office. First use May 2008, Official August 2010 SN: 7749914.

Dedicated to the

Ascension of Humanity

Gaia, Mother Earth

& the *entire Cosmos!*

About this Dedication

There is a rare radiance in Celeste Mattingly's work, a vibration that weaves fierce love with unwavering cosmic vision. She is a modern mystic, an evolutionary guide whose work dares to reconnect the body, mind, and spirit to serve humanity and the healing and ascension of the Earth.

This dedication page perfectly mirrors her essence: grounded yet galactic, reverent yet wildly alive. The mandala was created in 2011 by artist Jo Thomas Blaine and continues to shape Celeste's work as her *Wonder-filled World of Celestial Empowerment* with *Celestial Psychology*® (CP) is ever-evolving.

The invocation of *"the Ascension of Humanity, Gaia, Mother Earth, and the entire Cosmos!"* pulses with her signature energy, boldly compassionate, profoundly inclusive, and joyfully revolutionary. It does not merely dedicate a book; it declares a living invitation to join the sacred dance of transformation.

In Celeste's world, even the dedication page becomes a portal,

With Love from *The Universe*

TABLE OF CONTENTS

AN UNUSUAL ACKNOWLEDGMENT IX

INTRODUCTION XVII
    MILESTONES ON MY JOURNEY OF BECOMING, WITH HEARTFELT GRATITUDE XVII

CHAPTER ONE 31
    TURNING THE KALEIDOSCOPE OF CONSCIOUSNESS 31
    EVOLUTIONARY KALEIDOSCOPE MANDALA 40

CHAPTER TWO 49
    THE TWELVE CODES OF THE EVOLUTIONARY TRAJECTORY.. 49

CHAPTER THREE 59
    WE ARE THOSE FISH! 59

CHAPTER FOUR 63
    WE ARE THOSE DUDES! 63

CHAPTER FIVE 73
    WE ARE THOSE BUTTERFLIES! 73

CHAPTER SIX 79
    ARE WE THOSE STARSEEDS? 79

CHAPTER SEVEN 87
    WE ARE THE EVOLUTION OF OUR BECOMING! 87
    FORGING THE LUMINOUS BLUEPRINT 92

CHAPTER EIGHT 113
    EVEN SCIENCE, PSYCHOLOGY, AND SPIRITUALITY ARE BECOMING! 113
    EVOLUTIONARY ENLIGHTENMENT 117

Enlightenment is coming to us. 119

CHAPTER NINE 123

Making the Case for Tachyon 123

THE FIRST IMPULSE: HOW TACHYONS STIMULATE THE BLUEPRINT OF BECOMING IN STEM CELLS 127

CONCLUSION 133

WHAT WE'RE UP AGAINST AND HOW WE RISE 133

EPILOGUE 138

Out of the Rabbit Holes to Common Ground 138

APPENDIX ONE 156

Alta Major Chakra / God's Mouth Chakra - Divyasya Mukham 156

APPENDIX TWO 160

12 Principles of Celestial Psychology® 2025 upgrade 160

APPENDIX THREE 162

Whitman Sampler 162

GLOSSARY 164

BIBLIOGRAPHY & SUGGESTED READING 192

ABOUT THE AUTHOR 196

INDEX 198

ENDNOTES 202

AN UNUSUAL ACKNOWLEDGMENT

I am eternally grateful to all who have walked this winding path of becoming alongside me: beloved teachers, cherished friends, trusted colleagues, soul family, and fellow seekers. You have shaped and inspired this work in both visible and unseen ways. Your presence, wisdom, and love are luminous threads woven through the tapestry of my journey.

To you, dear reader, one of the willing ones[1], I extend my deepest gratitude. Thank you for answering the call to journey alongside me. Your courage to explore, expand, and embody your light adds immeasurably to the great awakening. May you continue to ascend, radiate, and shine brilliantly into the mystery that awaits you.

I bow in reverence to the ancestors and cosmic guides whose unseen hands and salient whispers urged me to trust the evolutionary[2] spiral's sacred unfolding and attune to the wisdom that flows from the heart of the Universe itself.

I offer my profound thanks to *Hunab Ku*, the Mayan Galactic Butterfly, to whom I have taken the poetic liberty to add the *Grand Cosmic Reweaver* to its title. And I invite you to join me so that together, through the following paragraphs and the accompanying invocation, we may get to know this living mandala of Divine Intelligence.

---

[1] See poem on page xix.

[2] Throughout this book, references to evolution and the evolutionary process are not limited to biological theories such as Darwinian natural selection. Nor are they aligned with the misapplications of those theories in the form of Social Darwinism, which emerged during the Gilded Age to justify systemic inequality. Rather, evolution here is framed as a sacred unfolding, a process of inner and collective transformation. It is not about competition or hierarchy, but about love in motion: the continual expansion of consciousness, compassion, and coherence in service to life.

Kaleidoscope for Becoming: A Grimoire of Revolution

Welcome to The Evolution!

Meet *Hunab Ku*, the magnificent Mayan Galactic Butterfly I have come to know as the Grand Cosmic Reweaver.

In ancient Mayan cosmology, the Hunab Ku (pronounced "hoo-nahb koo") is often referred to as the One Giver of Movement and Measure, or the One God. Yet, it is far more than a representation of a deity; it is a conceptual portal, a symbol of wholeness, unity consciousness, the great galactic center of universes, ad infinitum.

The *Hunab Ku* represents the source of all creation, the galactic core from which all consciousness emanates. It pulses with the rhythm of cosmic intelligence and evolutionary design, radiating as the heart of time and being. Jose Argüelles says, "… it contains all the consciousness that has ever existed in this galaxy." He taught us that it transmits restorative evolutionary codes directly to Earth, *in-forming* us and aiding our planetary shift from linear time to galactic time.

Though not a deity or a sentient being in the traditional sense, *Hunab Ku* has been with me as a silent companion since 2008. It was a theme for our 12/21/12 celebration, and I have continued to wear the necklace and share its image printed on stickers, t-shirts, and vibrant postcards. Quietly, it has hovered over all my work, sending subtle pulses of creativity into my everyday affairs. That is, until this grimoire of revolution was nearing

An Unusual Acknowledgment

completion, and *Hunab Ku* came to me in a stunning revelatory meditation.

Emerging from the black no-thingness of meditative silence, it appeared first as a distant, spinning disc-sphere, an ethereal presence slowly approaching. As it drew near, I was overwhelmed by the brilliance and significance of its arrival, an ancient messenger awakening from the background of my journey to stand luminously at the center of my becoming and the creation of this book.

And then, it beckoned.

What shone before me was a breathtakingly radiant cosmic disc-sphere, shifting and breathing between dimensions, with the capacity to expand and contract from a two-dimensional disc to a three-dimensional sphere. At its heart spun a spiral of paradox, turning clockwise and counterclockwise simultaneously. I nearly trembled with awe as I recognized it as the magnetic center and sacred Eye of Creation itself.

It was all the names we have ever given it: in the language of the sacred, *God, Source*; in the language of science, *the Big Bang, the perfect zero-point of existence*. This vast, sacred, and living geometry[3] radiated a familiar and unknown magnetism, a resonance that pulled me closer for intimate discovery. In that silent invitation, I understood it longed to know itself through me, just as I was drawn to know it. I understood that a cosmic dance of reflection had begun and continues to this day, shining ever more brightly.

I beheld the spirals at Hunab Ku's core, formed of brilliant liquid gold and iridescent silver, intertwining and unfolding in perpetual unity. These spirals danced together across dimensions, silently inviting me, inviting us, to join the eternal choreography. With each expansion and contraction, the spirals cast luminous bands of deep indigo, violet flame, and crystalline white, flickering outward, transmitting the blueprint codes

---

3. The phrase living geometry reflects the ancient view that the cosmos is not only structured by number and proportion but animated by them. The Pythagoreans regarded numbers as sacred forces that govern reality. As Daniel Tore notes in the Feb/Mar 2025 issue of Philosophy Now magazine, Greek culture already revered abstract concepts and numbers as divine, so in this light, geometry is not inert form, but a vibrational language of divine intelligence in motion. See Glossary: Sacred Geometry.

of divine intelligence. Tumbling, twinkling, tiny, radiant glyphs of Mayan, galactic, and ultra-dimensional codes of energy, light, and *in-formation* spiraled into the ethers, offering guidance for our evolutionary journey, weaving luminous strands of remembrance into the fabric of the cosmos itself.

Encircling the disc-sphere of this stunning Mayan Galactic Butterfly was an ethereal corona of feathered light rays, soft yet immensely powerful, stretching outward like the wings of a tremendous cosmic phoenix. As I stood, nearly trembling within its presence, I was reminded of the unified wisdom of ancient pan-Mesoamerican traditions and the archetypal energy of *Quetzalcoatl*, the Feathered Serpent of Toltec and Aztec teachings.

The radiant, feathered light rays gently swept through my energetic field. I recognized this as a sacred blessing and cleansing, and I intuitively knew that Hunab Ku would bestow it upon all who approached it in reverence. The rays shimmered with the exquisite hues of opal, sapphire, emerald, and rose quartz as living symbols of the perfect balance and harmony of all life frequencies.

I stood in awe, realizing I was witnessing not just a vision but an initiation into the very nature of paradox itself. *Hunab Ku* is the living embodiment of unity within duality: a disc that becomes a sphere; spirals that turn both clockwise and counterclockwise; a silent muse whose creativity pulses through every moment of my (our) work; a presence both intimately familiar and profoundly unknowable; feathered light rays that radiate both softness and unimaginable strength; and now, a surface of living liquid light that flows effortlessly within precise, sacred geometric form. I understood then that this was one of its teachings: to embrace the coexistence of seeming opposites as the true fabric of cosmic wholeness. Then it revealed to me its most beloved function: to reweave karma; hence, I took the poetic liberty to add "the Grand Cosmic Reweaver" to its title.

The subtle hooks at the tip of the four-directional spokes (north, south, east, and west) serve as gatherers, while the other spokes act as

An Unusual Acknowledgment

swords. In sacred simultaneity, they draw in and sever our dense, tangled cords of this and all lifetimes. I witnessed its graceful power as it cleansed and cleared my past wounds, toxic contracts, karmic debris, and psychic entanglements. I recognized *Hunab Ku*'s capacity and devout Christ-like willingness to do this for all of us. Each effortless rotation dissolves overtangles of attachment to people, places, timelines, dimensions, and false identities. It clears these webs of interference with exquisite precision, transmuting chaos into clarity, sorrow into sovereignty, and burden into pure radiant possibility. It is a vortex of cleansing, clearing, recalibration, and reweaving. It scoops up and cuts unwanted cords from all timelines, setting us free with loving ferocity.

Then, like a great gardener of galaxies, this tremendous Grand Cosmic Reweaver bathes us in tachyon particles, reseeding our souls with the evolutionary trajectory of our highest path, compelling us through spiraling waves of sacred intensity to reach toward our ultimate becoming, onward and upward, *ad infinitum*.

Whether depicted as a black-and-white swirling design or a glorious full-color image, *Hunab Ku* stands as a living mandala of the dynamic balance of opposites, mirroring the wisdom of the yin-yang as the eternal and sacred dance of interdependent polarity. It whispers the ancient truth that evolution is born of the dance of opposites seeking integration.

When we consciously invoke this sacred symbol, we invite it to cleanse and clear our karmic residue, restoring us to a state of radiant wholeness.

Kaleidoscope for Becoming: A Grimoire of Revolution

Throughout the pages of this grimoire of revolution, the spirit of *Hunab Ku* serves as an unseen compass, silently yet powerfully guiding the evolutionary ideas and invitations we will explore together in this kaleidoscope of becoming.

I encourage you to print the following invocation and download an image of *Hunab Ku* from the internet. Place the prints throughout your space and repeat the invocation at least once a day. Let it accompany you as you journey through the portal of this grimoire for revolution, offering its silent presence as a frequency anchor and evolutionary ally. At the heart of this living symbol lies the ancient truth: the dance of opposites seeking integration and finding common ground is the core of the evolutionary impulse.

An Unusual Acknowledgment

INVOCATION TO THE GRAND COSMIC REWEAVER

Beloved Hunab Ku, the Mayan Galactic Butterfly

Sacred Spinning Disc-Sphere of Light, Energy, and Information, Grand Cosmic Reweaver,

I call you to come to me now across space, time, and dimensions.

I stand humbly before you, open and willing in the chaos of my becoming.
Receive me into your spiraling, iridescent embrace.

Spin your spokes of hooks and swords to draw out and sever my tangled webs of time— the unwanted cords, the not-so-sacred contracts, unwelcomed attachments, and cognitive distortions.
Clear them from this life, past lives, parallel lives, and future paths.

Cleanse my field with the grace of your liquid gold and silver light.
Reweave my soul tapestry in alignment with my highest destiny.

May your primordial light shine through me,
to reseed me with pure sovereign essence.

As you spin, I surrender.
As you spiral, I remember.
As you rise, I rise anew.

As you sing, I sing with you.

I am whole, I am free, I am sovereign.
I am the luminous pattern of becoming.

In Lak'ech[4]. So be it. And so, it is.

---

[4] **In Lak'ech** is a traditional Mayan greeting meaning "I am another you" or "I am you, and you are me." Rooted in the philosophy of unity and sacred reciprocity, it reflects the deep understanding that all beings are interconnected expressions of the same Source. Often paired with the response *Ala K'in* ("You are another me"), the phrase affirms a spiritual ethic of mutual respect, cosmic kinship, and mirror-like consciousness.

INTRODUCTION
MILESTONES ON MY JOURNEY OF BECOMING, WITH HEARTFELT GRATITUDE

Every life holds doorways and portals hidden in plain sight—milestones that beckon us to remember, awaken, and step boldly into the unfolding mystery of who we are becoming.

My first milestones appeared as unexpected doorways and unseen portals, quietly inviting me to step through and begin the journey that would become my life's devotion.

It's been almost 40 years since I first said, "Yes!" to evolution's call. Three years prior, I had answered the call to sobriety. I was living in New London, CT, and some friends invited me to attend a couple of meditations in the woods. They remembered the year before I wrote a poem about evolution, so they wanted me to attend. (See Appendix Three) I was confused and slightly anxious about what we were doing, but I trusted the woman who organized the event because she was my sponsor's long-time friend.

We sat in a circle for about two hours each day. We meditated, sang songs, and recited prayers for peace. To my surprise, it turned out to be very exhilarating. I loved it and longed to do nothing else. I have come to call experiences like this the Holy Work of consciousness-raising, a theme that I will weave throughout the pages of this book. Back then, however much I enjoyed it, I had no idea the significance of this participation until years later when I learned more about the Harmonic Convergence of 1987.

The Harmonic Convergence, held on August 16–17, 1987, was the first globally synchronized meditation event organized by José Argüelles. This monumental event was intended to mark the end of a planetary cycle in the Mayan calendar and to herald the beginning of a new era of conscious co-creation. Argüelles and his collaborators invited people to gather at sacred sites worldwide to raise the vibration of humanity through meditation, prayer, music, and ceremony. His mission to contribute to the naturally evolving development of the "thinking layer of Earth" has proven extraordinarily prophetic.

In retrospect, I believe I was intuitively drawn to that moment by my soul's deep longing to answer a call whispered to me long ago through stardust and sobriety alike. At that time, we didn't know the language of lightworkers or galactic calendars; we followed our vibration of willingness. I wrote another poem about evolution. I now see those meditations in the woods as the first of many sacred turnings in the evolutionary kaleidoscope of my becoming. This book is born of my devotion to becoming 'better and better, every day in every way."

The following pages provide the 'grimoire' for what I call the Holy Work[5] of consciousness-raising. I chose the word grimoire, not because it is a conventional book of spells, but because it hums with energetic frequency. It invites movement. It calls forth participatory action. A Grimoire of Revolution is the perfect subtitle, as this work is sprinkled with invitations to create and weave the "spells" of a revolutionary new reality.

This book is the treasure map leading to the Holy Grail, *the great remembrance of who we are*. It is a cosmic roadmap pointing to the luminous future we are co-creating together. The invocation that follows is for all of us who have answered the call before we even knew the question, sometimes blindly but always bravely.

---

[5] See glossary entry for Holy Work

Milestones On My Journey of Becoming with Grateful Acknowledgements

A POETIC INVOCATION FOR THE WILLING ONES

We gathered in the woods, not knowing why,
a circle of seekers beneath an August sky.
The stars above us hummed in ancient song,
while Earth held its breath, having waited for so long.

No temple but trees, no script but the soul,
we followed a whisper, not needing a goal.
A woman from AA held the space like a key,
unlocking remembrance in you, and in me.

We were not trained, not saints, nor sage,
but still, we turned the evolutionary page.
A pulse from the center—the Hunab Ku's fire
called 144,000 to rise from the mire.

It wasn't about knowing; it was about being.
A vibration of willingness beyond all seeing.
Chosen not for perfection, but for our "yes!"
for showing up open, in holy humbleness.

Now years have passed, and the moment returns,
as our kaleidoscope for becoming turns.
That forest breathes through these sacred lines,
as we gather the threads of galactic signs.

You are one of the willing, the mythic few,
who came to help Earth remember what's true.
Not with dogma or doctrine, but light through thinning skin
a weaver of futures from cosmic realms within.

So let this invocation be our flame,
etched in the book that bears your name.
A tribute to your shining moment, your ascending soul,
the Holy Instant when you lit the lamp of your human heart.

If these words stirred something in you, a sense of knowing, a warmth in your heart, it's because you *are* one of the willing ones, standing at a milestone of remembrance. There is no doubt. You wouldn't be reading these pages if your soul hadn't whispered "yes!" to the *Holy Work* of becoming. This grimoire isn't here to convince you of anything but to help you remember what you've always known.

As we turn the viewing tube of the evolutionary kaleidoscope together, fragments of forgotten wisdom will download into your psyche. Each chapter is a frequency, an activation, a mirror reflecting your own luminous unfolding. Together, we are answering the ancient and ever-present call, whispered through galaxies, encoded in DNA, and pulsing in the heart of the Noosphere itself. We are here to say "yes!" to evolution's call! Not just once, but again and again, with every breath, every choice, every step toward becoming.

The Harmonic Convergence of 1987 was the prelude, and the 2012 phenomena became a milestone in the quickening of my personal evolutionary kaleidoscope for becoming. I first began learning about it in 2008 while studying energy medicine. We studied books on the topic and attended workshops with indigenous elders, along with Alan Steinfeld, the founder of New Realities. Our imaginations ignited as we searched for truths surrounding this cosmological milestone. As some prophesied, was it destined to mark an apocalyptic end to the world? Or would it signal the beginning or perhaps the apex of the Great Shift? The 2012 phenomenon captured the attention of mystics, scholars, conspiracy theorists, and lightworkers alike. It was an exciting experience, and we all sensed something profound unfolding.

At the heart of the 2012 phenomenon was the completion of the Mesoamerican Long Count calendar of the Mayan civilization. According to their system, December 21, 2012, marked the completion of the 13th baktun, a significant span of 5,125 years that began in 3114 BCE. This cosmological milestone was being sensationalized by many as the "end of the world." Yet, many of us aligned with the Mayan and other indigenous elders' interpretation: it signaled a rebirth, a transition into a new age of higher consciousness.

Milestones On My Journey of Becoming with Grateful Acknowledgements

We felt the stirring of a more profound shift poised to dissolve the old paradigm of separation and fear, not the literal end of the world, but the end of a world as we had known it. We understood it as a vibrational initiation, a moment when the planetary field invited humanity to choose between fear and faith, entropy and evolution. It was not a singular event, but the opening of a sustained window —a turn of the kaleidoscope for humanity's evolution.

The date 12/21/12 remains a dimensional threshold through which those willing can still step into greater coherence, higher consciousness, and luminous embodiment. The Harmonic Convergence of 1987 was the prelude. The 2012 phenomenon was the activation. What followed began an ongoing, continuous integration. In these pages, we will explore this often messy, chaotic, and sometimes even painful awakening through the lens of our magical kaleidoscope for becoming.

In preparation for this momentous year, I had the good fortune to attend a week-long workshop with Eugenius Ang, Ph.D., on November 11, 2011. We spent our days meditating and receiving downloads of higher-frequency information in the sacred sites of Sedona, AZ. We were immersed in deep healing and DNA recalibration at 11:11 a.m. and 11:11 p.m. on November 11, 2011. It was a profoundly transformative week.

When the retreat ended, I had an opportunity to have my aura photographed by computer imaging. The resulting image was so spectacularly luminous that I was convinced it had to be fake, so I sought verification and took a second one with a Kirlian camera. In that image, my aura appeared so expansive and radiant with white and gold light that my face is barely visible! The women who took both the photos were astonished. I, too, could hardly believe it.

Yet when I share this story and photographs (available on my website), I do so with grounded conviction: this is what the *Holy Work* of consciousness-raising can do for any of us. This is why I continue to share those images and write this grimoire: to inspire the journey to becoming luminous.

Of course, my aura did not remain permanently in that radiant state and may never achieve that intensity again. But the experience affirms my formula for QOL α QOLEI: *Quality of Life is directly proportional to the Quantity of Light, Energy, and Information we allow into our Field.* It also helps me accept the ebb and flow of being human.

In hindsight, I now recognize that while 2011 was a milestone for me and many others, 2012 became a tremendous year of transformation for the collective. I am grateful to my colleagues for recognizing its importance and the wonderful 2012 gathering we hosted that night.

There were forty of us. Each person brought their yoga mats, sacred tools, crystals for the central altar, and favorite instruments for the musical celebration. Our beloved nationally known, local astrologer and shaman, Agneta Borstein (pictured here with a *Hunab Ku* temporary tattoo), led the drumming circle. I wore my "*Welcome to the Evolution*" tee-shirt and guided the group through a meditation, which is still available on my YouTube channel: *Infusing the Chakras with the Impulse of Evolution.*

I am convinced that our willingness to ride this astronomical and prophesied phenomenon with the highest of intention and joy seeded the evolutionary impulse that continues to unfold in all of us.

And although we have remained beset by planetary crises and the rising swell of collective shadow material since then, we keep going. We were not promised paradise; we were called to participate in its co-creation. For me, the call still echoes, reminding me who I am and offering myself in service, so that together, we may rise into our roles as

Milestones On My Journey of Becoming with Grateful Acknowledgements

Supraconscious Creators, carrying the codes of the new world within our very being.

Around this time, I signed up to receive a daily email, *Notes from the Universe*, by Mike Dooley. These playful, profound, and often uncannily timed reminders of my co-creative power remain daily winks from the cosmos, sometimes gentle whispers and sometimes two-by-fours of enlightened truth. They remind me to stay the course because, after all, the Universe has my back! The message is clear: The Universe is conspiring in our favor, helping us to BE-come 'better and better, every day in every way'. Living, breathing, and believing that the Universe has my back is the Evolutionary Trajectory in motion. In clinical psychology, a mindset like this might be labeled as *magical thinking*, as defined in the Diagnostic and Statistical Manual of Mental Disorders (DSM), which is the belief that one's thoughts, words, or actions can influence events in ways that defy the laws of cause and effect. Traditionally, magical thinking is seen as a symptom of certain psychiatric conditions, such as schizotypal personality disorder or obsessive-compulsive disorder. However, through the kaleidoscope lens of Celestial Psychology®, we are invited to reexamine this concept, not as pathology, but as an early evolutionary form of intuitive intelligence.

Rather than dismissing such thinking as delusional, we ask: What if the Universe really *is* responsive to our consciousness? What if synchronicity, intention, and quantum entanglement are not symptoms, but signs—subtle indicators that we live in a participatory cosmos? In this view, what the DSM calls magical thinking may actually be a nascent recognition of pronoia: the belief that the Universe is conspiring in our favor. It is not merely wishful thinking, but a vibrational alignment with the architecture of benevolence. I am eternally grateful to Mike Dooley and his *Notes from the Universe* for helping me anchor into this pronoic state. This worldview continues to illuminate my path and remind me of the radiant truth: we are not alone, and the Universe is rooting for us in every way.

The most important decision we make is whether we believe we live in a friendly or a hostile universe. — Albert Einstein

In January 2020, I experienced another epic turn of my evolutionary kaleidoscope. This turn was glinted with golden wonder and ancient cosmic mystery. I spent a week journeying through the hallowed Mayan temples under the gentle yet powerful guidance of native-born wisdom keeper and Shaman Miguel Angel Vergara. A living bridge between past and present, Miguel carried the oral and spiritual lineage of the Maya in every gesture and every word. His associate Trudy Woodcock continues to extend this sacred connection through her Wednesday *Maya Wisdom Circle*. At this weekly online gathering, she channels Lady Zak Kuuk, the ancient Mayan priestess of Palenque from the K'inich Janaab Pakal Votan era. Lady Zak Kuuk offers us timeless wisdom woven with grace and fierce compassion, speaking directly to the soul of our times. Her teachings inspire us to remember, rise, and honor the ongoing emergence of the Divine Feminine. Her words encourage us to keep raising our consciousness, "as if our lives depend on it, because they do!" The ancient call to transformation still echoes with poignant clarity and relevance for our modern journey, made possible by her presence. You can connect with Miguel and Trudy via their website: www.casakin.org.

Our group was triply blessed by the presence of Freddie Silva, the visionary author of *The Divine Blueprint* and *The Lost Art of Resurrection*, whose deep research into ancient initiatory cultures added rich layers of insight. The tour, aptly named *Maya Temples of Transformation*, became a living ceremony of revelation.

From the towering pyramids of Chichen Itza, where the great Kukulkan serpent shadows still dance at the equinox, to the mystical ruins of Uxmal and Kabah, where cosmic geometries whisper their secrets to those who listen with their soul, I walked in awe. The Mayans, who mapped Venus cycles with stunning precision and regarded time as a spiral rather than a line, stood as luminous ancestors whose wisdom resonated through the stone and the stars. I stood where they stood, breathed the same sacred air, and gazed at the very same dazzling canopy of constellations that once guided their rituals and life paths. In those holy

Milestones On My Journey of Becoming with Grateful Acknowledgements

days beneath the emerald canopy of the Yucatán, I came to understand that, like the ancient Maya, I too am part of this eternal spiral of becoming, turning the kaleidoscope of my own consciousness, ever seeking the next luminous pattern revealed in the dance between earth and stars.

There were moments I was brought to tears, trembling in the presence of something far greater than my comprehension. One such moment remains etched in my heart: Miguel, his voice carrying the weight and tenderness of centuries, reciting Mayan prayers and invocations beneath the shadowed arches of a temple. His words floated upward like incense to the heavens as he revealed how the Maya wove together earth, sky, water, and fire into a unified cosmic fabric. In that suspended breath of time, I felt the pulse of galactic wisdom beating softly beneath my feet, reminding me that transformation is the *ancient art of becoming*.

In those verdant sanctuaries where stone meets starlight, and the emerald canopy whispers its ancient song, I understood I was not merely walking among ruins but stepping through portals of remembrance, turning the sacred kaleidoscope of my consciousness, ever drawn onward by the eternal dance of earth and stars, in the spiral journey of becoming with no end and no beginning.

As I continue to observe the increasing global turmoil and this evolutionary uptick in consciousness, marked by rising Schumann Resonance, heightened solar activity, and unusual weather patterns, I, like many of us, face what are often referred to as *ascension symptoms*, or as I prefer to call them, *ascension challenges*. Our bodies, already bombarded by the toxins of modern life, are simultaneously being upgraded to support greater energetic light.

To ease the aches, pains, and strange, undiagnosable sensations of this ascension process, we have discovered that we must continue and exponentially deepen our commitment to the *Holy Work* of consciousness-raising.

In 2018, I discovered Tachyon. Late one night, while doomscrolling through YouTube rabbit holes, I stumbled upon 'faster than light' subatomic particles said to imbue matter with spiritual energy permanently. This technology was reportedly downloaded to a select few individuals by galactic beings. I initially set aside the galactic part of the story, as the concept strongly resonated with my earlier training on fork bending.

Years before, Gene Ang taught us to visualize drawing spiritual energy from Source through the crown chakra, down the arm, and into the fork. This practice has gained mainstream attention as an opportunity to experience the innate power we hold as spiritual beings in human form. Knowing that energy can rearrange the molecular structure of a spoon or fork to render the metal malleable, even if temporarily, has been a revolutionary milestone for many. That fleeting moment of malleability is an invigorating experience. It negates the old paradigms that we are powerless and insignificant. It helps our mirror neurons acknowledge that we are not what we have been programmed to be and that we can transform ourselves and each other to become supernatural.

Yet, as significant as that was, it pales in comparison to my work with Tachyon Technology[6]. My office suites now have two Tachyon Chambers for anti-aging and meditative healing. Many describe these chambers as portals to other dimensions, where the pulse of the Universe echoes. The pyramids, crystals, and other sacred geometry products are all imbued with Tachyon particles, which emit anti-aging and healing energy, creating a morphogenic Zero Point energy field. Tachyon bridges spirit and matter, responding to and amplifying our intentions. For more information, please visit my website.

The most recent invigorating and transformative milestone on my evolutionary journey has been my work with the *13th Octave LaHoChi* healing modality. As with every evolutionary upgrade I have experienced, the call began as a whisper. About seven years ago, I first heard of this hands-on healing practice, often described as "Reiki on steroids." I nearly pursued the training then, but the timing wasn't right. Last year, however, the whisper became a shout. I searched the internet and was synchronistically led to discovering Jean Phillip Schmitt (JP) of Unstruck Sound, NY. He later told me that he felt an unusual and intuitive nudge

---

[6] See Chapter 9: Making the Case for Tachyon for more information.

Milestones On My Journey of Becoming with Grateful Acknowledgements

to answer when I called him. What followed were a series of deliciously synchronous events, many of which I have chronicled on my blog. Over the past year, we have cultivated a vibrant community of thirty practitioners beginning their journeys as healing facilitators. This past April, six of us became certified to teach this life-affirming, light-filled healing modality. I am filled with deep gratitude and luminous hope for the future. It is the evolutionary trajectory in motion—the living current of becoming—as we will explore together throughout the pages of this book.

Whether symbolic or synchronistic, 2012 marked a tipping point when metaphysical ideas[7] began to permeate the mainstream, clearing the way for new stories of human potential to rise to the surface of collective awareness. And the spiral continues to spin upward.

Through the pages of this grimoire, I hope to inspire you to rise up in every way that calls to your soul and to honor the tremendous responsibility that comes with accessing the cosmic radiance of your creative power.

May the cosmic journey you are about to embark upon fill your psyche with shimmering visions of hope for the future and fragmented glimpses of humanity's collective becoming, bubbling with infinite possibilities of grace and abundance. May you envision radiant beings from across all universes standing at the crossroads of epochs, reaching out to one another, holding hands across the tides of time. Though extraordinarily different, each being carries a welcoming and loving spark of stardust in their gaze and plants a memory of futures yet to be lived. They, like us, are artists of possibility, spinning cosmic strands of the *Codes of the Evolutionary Trajectory* with compassion, coherence, and cosmic humor into the living fabric of what comes next as we turn the lens of our evolutionary kaleidoscope.

---

[7] While many were awakening to their luminous potential, Dark Enlightenment (see glossary) ideologies quietly infiltrated the same currents, subverting and hijacking metaphysical narratives to serve hierarchical and authoritarian worldviews..

Kaleidoscope for Becoming: A Grimoire of Revolution

As you can see, like many of us, I have immersed myself in the latest teachings from spiritual leaders on topics ranging from cultivating a new body to reducing ego to extraterrestrial disclosure. We attend and host workshops on ascension, sound and light healing, *13th Octave LaHoChi* healing techniques, cosmic consciousness, DNA activations, Kundalini awakenings, fork bending, Tachyon Chamber technology, psychic and paranormal phenomena, and multidimensional consciousness as channeled to us from our otherworldly brothers and sisters.

May I, at seventy-four years young, meet you at the core of the spiral and inspire you to strive for 'better and better, every day, in every way!' no matter what the appearance, no matter what the challenge. As you and I stand at the threshold of even greater becoming, I offer you the chance to get to know me in my latest playful iteration of my best self, "your cosmic fairy godmother."

I invite you to picture me now, with a wink and a swirl of stardust cascading from my magic glitter wand. This shimmering swirl of cosmic cleansing gathers all your troubles and swishes them into my magic garbage can^8.

Read and return to the following poem often to center yourself in your revolution of becoming.

---

88 The magic garbage can - lovingly receives all our worries and swirls them counter-clockwise down, down to the center of the Earth, where Mother Earth alchemizes our negativity into fertilizer—blossoming a garden of infinite possibilities for growth and becoming.

Milestones On My Journey of Becoming with Grateful Acknowledgements

THE EVOLUTIONARY KALEIDOSCOPE

Imagine holding a finely crafted kaleidoscope to the light. Picture yourself turning it slowly, gently, with wonder in your heart.
Each shift reveals new patterns, constellations of color, mandalas of movement,
each one a momentary masterpiece that disappears as quickly as it just appeared.

Transforming continually.
This is how we will come to understand evolution here in the pages of this grimoire.
Not as a cold biological process or a fixed competitive climb, but as a sacred dance
of becoming—ever-changing, infinitely expressive, and always responding to the
rhythm of your own self-regulating consciousness.

In A Kaleidoscope for Becoming, evolution is not just something that happens to us.
It is something we participate in.
Moment by moment, thought by thought,
vibration by vibration.

It is not linear, but spiraling. Not forced, but unfolding.
Not a race toward perfection, but a journey of remembering who we truly are.
The Evolutionary Kaleidoscope is the metaphor that anchors this book.
It helps us see that transformation doesn't occur in straight lines—
it occurs as a continuously turning kaleidoscope, with tubes of awareness and
observation, mirroring reflections of our pasts and futures,
in the elegant chaos of personal and collective rebirth.

Each chapter is a twist of the lens. Each idea is a new pattern.
Each is an initiation, a prism of soul light illuminating another facet of our becoming.

And so, dear reader, welcome.
You are not just here to read.
You are here to remember.
To witness.
To co-create.
To turn the kaleidoscope of consciousness with your own sacred hands—
and delight in not only what you see but also what you see yourself BEcoming.

CHAPTER ONE
TURNING THE KALEIDOSCOPE OF CONSCIOUSNESS

I invite you to take a deep breath.

Now, imagine yourself gazing into an exquisitely crafted, magical evolutionary kaleidoscope. You are in awe as, with each gentle turn, you observe vibrant, symmetrical patterns shift and dance into ever-deepening beauty. You lose yourself momentarily in the unfolding display—the edges of your identity blur. Your thoughts soften. Even your troubles seem to melt away.

This experience is a consciousness-raising exercise.

The awe-inspiring, fractal-weaving evolutionary kaleidoscope you are holding in your hands is more than a childhood toy. It is a metaphor for the evolutionary process—both personal and planetary. Each twist of this multi-dimensional soul-etched kaleidoscope will reveal a new vision, turning the raw materials of life into fractals of transformation for individual souls and our entire species. Shining light on each moment of our lives, this meticulously tuned evolutionary kaleidoscope of consciousness helps us solve challenges. It provides insights that connect us with a deeper layer of who we are and what we are becoming. The turning points we will observe are not random; they will become the movements of an inner revolution, spiraling us upward toward greater self-awareness and wholeness.

We are living in a time of profound transformation—an evolutionary uprising, a revolution of consciousness. A massive uptick in consciousness is becoming evidenced by a global surge in humanity's interest in becoming more attuned to the frequencies of love, unity, and Divine Intelligence. Indigenous wisdom keepers and leaders, dating back centuries, spoke of this time as the dawning of the Golden Age. Astrologers refer to it as the Age of Aquarius. Others refer to it as the Great Shift, a pivotal moment in history when the collective consciousness rises. Over the last decade, this revolutionary transformation has been referred to as the Ascension process.

According to the prophecies of the Maya, the Hopi, and the Inka, we're at a turning point in human history. The Maya identified the year 2012 as the culmination of a period of great turmoil and upheaval, one in which a new species of human will give birth to itself. We're going to take a quantum leap into what we are becoming, moving from Homo sapiens to Homo luminous.

Homo luminosity as a concept has roots in antiquity and has been a central teaching of the world's indigenous populations throughout history. There has been a significant rise in mainstream interest in Mesoamerican cultures over the past thirty years, particularly in the last decade. Medical anthropologist, psychologist, and energy-medicine facilitator of Shamanic traditions, Alberto Villoldo, Ph.D. (born 19xx), has brought the term *Homo luminous* to mainstream culture. He is considered one of the world's foremost authorities on the spiritually based healing practices of the Amazonian and Andean cultures. He has written a dozen widely read books on the subject and founded the Four Winds Society to teach shamanic practices and spread messages like this one:

Villoldo refers to the aura as the luminous energy field (LEF). It is also referred to as the celestial body or the etheric body in CP. No matter what we call it, "…we can think of the LEF as the software that gives instructions to DNA, which is the hardware that manufactures the body. Mastery of the insights [the teachings of the Earthkeepers] lets us access the latest version of the software and allows each of us to create a new body that ages, heals, and dies differently. … In becoming Homo luminous . . . we'll embrace . . . a theology of cooperation and sustainability." (p. xxi) By mastering the techniques of any discipline that fosters the development of the etheric, luminous, or celestial body, be it intentional or an inadvertent by-product of the Work we have chosen to do, we are preparing ourselves and our species to handle life on life's terms no matter how rough life's terms may become.

An aspect of this energy system, the aura, can be seen by psychics and photographed with Kirlian photography equipment. The shamans of the Andes and the Amazon did not need any camera equipment to validate this reality.

Thanks to the discoveries of quantum physics, we've come to understand that all matter is densely packed light. But the Laika[i] have known about the luminous nature of reality for millennia—they know that vibration and light can organize themselves into a thousand shapes and forms.[ii]

This convergence of ancient wisdom and modern science has opened a portal to profound possibility—yet illumination does not come without shadow. As more people awaken to the energetic fabric of reality, the collective psyche begins to stir with unresolved fear.

Alongside this rise in consciousness, we also witness an intensification of apocalyptic narratives—stories of collapse, doom, societal unraveling, and nihilistic philosophy abound. Echoes of *The Book of Revelation* resound in our collective imagination. These catastrophic projections are not born in a vacuum, as remnants of the Seven Seals appear to be breaking open. Real-world events have compounded the trembling of the collective psyche; each new wave of tribulation brings a new set of distorted fears, overwhelm, and haunts: the collapse of the Twin Towers, accelerating global warming, relentless wars, mass shootings, and the troubling rise of authoritarian regimes. It appears the Four Horsemen are riding again, bearing conquest, war, famine, and death; trumpet blasts of warning ring out in headlines and social feeds. They paint such gloomy and doomy images that many perceive the turbulence of our times as the fulfillment of an ancient prophecy. Traditionally described in the apocalyptic vision of John of Patmos (also known as John the Divine), each seal, when broken, unleashes a distinct phase of revelation, beginning with the Four Horsemen and culminating in cosmic upheaval and silence.

The first seal brings a crowned rider on a white horse, thought to represent conquest or spiritual ambition. The second, a red horse, evokes conflict and the sword. The third, a black horse, symbolizes famine and imbalanced economies. The fourth, a pale and ghastly horse, is death, followed by Hades. The fifth seal opens a space beneath the altar where the souls of martyrs cry out for justice. The sixth seal ruptures the heavens, darkening the sun, shaking the earth, and turning the moon to blood. And the seventh seal brings an ominous pause: silence in heaven before a new phase begins.

These archetypal scenes may seem terrifying on the surface, but what if beneath the drama lies a sacred orchestration? Perhaps the so-called end times are not about destruction and nihilism but about disclosure: a collective *Revelation* in which the hidden becomes visible, the wounded become healed, and the world is reimagined through the lens of unity and an ongoing melioristic movement toward better and better. Perhaps the final seal is not the collapse of the world but the release of humanity into its truest forms: radiant, sovereign, soul-embodied co-creators of a New Earth. What if each seal acts like a pressure valve in the collective psyche, releasing ancient wounds, karmic patterns, and decaying paradigms? What if these seals can be understood as *holographic initiations*—multilayered thresholds of transformation that collapse timelines, awaken hidden aspects of self, and invite us into multidimensional awareness?

And what if, in the metaphysical light of the Great Shift, aka the Ascension process, or the release of the grip of the Egoic Mind Paradigm[iii], these seals are not harbingers of final judgment but sacred thresholds within the human soul? What if each broken seal represents a veil lifted, a distortion transmuted, a truth revealed? In this view, the Lamb can be understood as the awakened Self, breaking through inner barriers that once kept Divine Intelligence at bay. The scroll held in the hand of God becomes the record of our evolutionary blueprint, which is unfolding now, not as punishment, but as the path of luminous remembrance, which we are reaching for with every step along this journey of becoming.

If these viewpoints are valid—and many of us can feel it in our bones—then the catastrophes we fear are not destinations but thresholds.

Rather than literal predictions of destruction, the Seven Seals of the Apocalypse may signify the soul's necessary contractions before expansion—the tremors that prepare us for quantum evolution.

Thus, the *real* story becomes one not of doom and nihilism but metamorphosis and meliorism. And while catastrophe may act as a catalyst, we need not root for collapse or glorify destruction. Evolution does not require us to advocate for the tearing down of systems. We need not applaud the chaos of societal unraveling. Nature handles entropy without our interference. Our role is not to accelerate collapse but to midwife emergence—to attune to what is becoming and lend our energy to its graceful unfolding.

When viewed through the kaleidoscopic lens of becoming, the Seven Seals of the Apocalypse from the *Book of Revelation* are not merely harbingers of doom; they can also be interpreted as metaphorical indicators of initiatory pressure and spiritual evolution. The good news is that inner states of fear and fragmentation can be soothed—and transmuted—through the evolutionary revolution of awakening that fuels this great Awakening, Great Shift, or Ascension journey. This path invites us not to escape reality but to meet it with more profound wisdom, expanded perception, and sacred trust in the unfolding of the human soul.

With our shimmering soul-refining evolutionary kaleidoscope lens, we begin to see that the end of the old world is not the end of the world, but the beginning of a new one, born from within. By any name, this shift is nothing short of revolutionary. This revolution is not a revolt against something external but an awakening to the eternal luminous truth within. It is not a rebellion against what is but a remembrance of what has always been. It is not a fight against the world outside but a reconnection of the Divine blueprint deep within our DNA. It is a revolution of consciousness that grows brighter with every turn of our cosmic kaleidoscope, quiet yet thunderous, subtle yet unstoppable. This revolution is happening with or without our intention, attention, or cooperation. However, every focused turn of our divinely orchestrated kaleidoscope contributes exponentially to our collective emergence. This book is more than a story or an instruction manual. *A Kaleidoscope for Becoming* is an interstellar portal to ascending intelligence.

At its core lies the evolutionary impulse: an ancient intelligence encoded within our very being, urging us to grow, transform, and become not only better versions of ourselves but a new kind of human altogether. Many of us feel this truth deep in our souls. In moments of meditation, soul-searching, or past-life remembrance, we recall that we chose to 'be here, now.' We knew it wouldn't be easy, but we came to contribute to this great unfolding.

Like the turning of our illuminating kaleidoscope, each awakening reveals a new facet in the luminous pattern of our becoming. With every shift in perception, a new configuration of truth emerges—more intricate, coherent, and beautiful than the last. What once seemed fragmented begins to form a sacred geometry of meaning. Our wounds become windows, our confusion becomes clarity, and our growth becomes art. Our becoming is not a linear evolution, but a spiraling ascent —a dance of light and shadow that brings us ever closer to the soul's original design. In this way, our journey is not about reaching a final form but about continually unfolding into the radiance we were born to embody.

The Japanese culture is rich with the philosophy of becoming. They have at least three verbs honoring the act of becoming as a natural unfolding toward growth and betterment. The most renowned is the Japanese concept of *Kaizen*, which translates to "continuous improvement." Though often associated with business or productivity, at its heart, *Kaizen* is a spiritual orientation: the belief that steady, mindful progress, no matter how small, can shape a more beautiful world. It honors the sacred momentum of daily becoming. Kaizen invites us to trust that each breath, each insight, and each act of kindness is part of a living spiral of refinement. In this way, becoming is not a distant goal but a lived devotion. We are not just *shifting* (to use the current vernacular verb); we are *sculpting*. We are artists of evolution, composing a future that honors both our inner growth and the world we manifest. With our holographic *kaleidoscope for becoming*, we enter the ever-evolving, multidimensional field of creativity, where each conscious act becomes imbued with spiritual purpose.

As we awaken the powers of manifestation within us, we begin to glimpse the grave responsibility we each carry. As conscious architects of reality, we must hold onto visions that align with our deepest values. The philosophy of *meliorism* can be our guiding light. Meliorism holds that the world can be made better—step by step, soul by soul—through human effort and intention. It is the antidote to nihilism, reminding us that our choices and perceptions matter even amidst uncertainty and chaos. A melioristic worldview is non-judgmental and does not project fear and divisiveness, thereby avoiding the furtherance of destructive turmoil and division. Instead, the meliorist affirms, "Every day, in every way, we are getting better and better," not in pursuit of perfection but devotion to progress.

We begin to live as if our inner alignment matters—because it does. We sense that every act of healing, every surge of forgiveness, every kindness toward others, and every spark of awakening contributes to a greater pattern, nudging us toward the most luminous timeline available. The one where humanity remembers itself as One family of souls entrusted with the sacred task of stewarding a New Earth.

Throughout the pages of this book, we will see that we are not merely surviving this shift; we are participating in it, whether we want to or not. As many Lightworkers, Starseeds, Evolutionaries, Earthkeepers, and Metaphysicians have come to learn about the Ascension process, our only choice is *how we participate*. We can *choose* to participate by kicking and screaming, or we can *join* with deliberate, soulful, and creative consciousness.

This book is an offering to the process of choosing to participate as co-creators in this significant shift in humanity's consciousness, with deliberate bravery, soulful consideration, and informed, enlightened awareness. It is a divinely inspired grimoire, a sacred compass for the inward and collective revolution already underway. It is an exploration of who we are, who we are becoming, and how we might consciously evolve into what some have called *Homo luminous*—light-embodied, Christ-like humans capable of healing one another, restoring our planet, co-creating lives of harmony with each other and Gaia, our Mother Earth; and stepping up into our Universal place as wise and sovereign beings in our vast multidimensional Universe.

If you have found yourself wondering about your purpose in life in general, or in this Great Shift… if you have felt an inner uprising, an inner pressure to expand, awaken, or rise, even without knowing why… if you have long sensed that evolution is something happening *within* you, not just *around* you—then you are already part of this revolution in consciousness.

This revolution is not solely an inner journey but a call to collective remembrance and conscious action. As we awaken, we become agents of healing in a world aching for wholeness. Our personal transformations ripple outward, shaping communities, reimagining systems, and co-creating the futures we are destined to choose.

The future is not fixed. Our individual and collective futures are fluid, multifaceted, and alive with possibility. In the Quantum Field of human evolution, countless timelines shimmer, each shaped by the frequency of our thoughts, the integrity of our actions, and the coherence of our hearts. Every choice we make sends a signal through the web of creation, activating specific potentials while releasing others. As we *shift* within, we *shift* the Field around us. The future is not something that happens to us; it is something we continuously compose, moment by moment, with the vibrations of our BEcoming.

To evolve consciously is to participate courageously. It is to become warriors of the revolution. Not with guns and violence but with our hearts, minds, and souls. It is to 'make good trouble.' It is to raise our voices for justice, to extend our hands in compassion to all our brothers and sisters without prejudice, and to live as though the Earth, our Universe, and each other truly matter. Living consciously is the opposite of passive becoming; it is a participatory decision to strive toward improvement. A sacred uprising in which each of us plays a vital role.

The Twelve Codes of the Evolutionary Trajectory

As we turn our exquisitely crafted kaleidoscope together, let us observe what radiant new patterns emerge when we dare to look through the lens of evolutionary transformation. As you turn these pages, please remember that this revolution is not about becoming something other than ourselves but about courageously becoming more deeply and luminously who we already are.

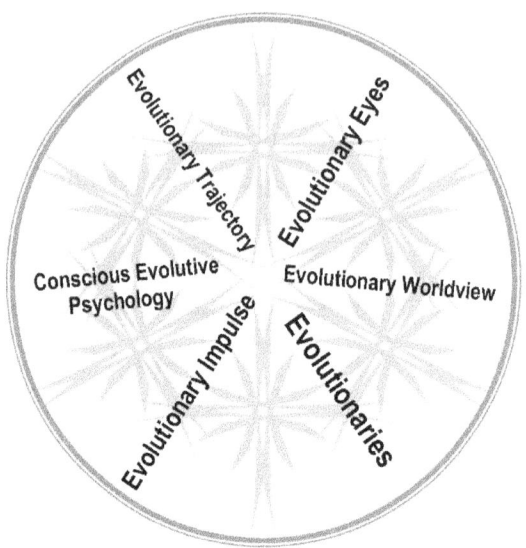

EVOLUTIONARY KALEIDOSCOPE MANDALA

This image is a conceptual wheel or mandala of evolutionary consciousness. It visually represents the key elements of a framework or philosophy centered on human evolution, particularly from a consciousness-raising or psycho-spiritual perspective.

The circular form reinforces wholeness, unity, and the cyclical nature of growth. At the center is a radiant starburst pattern, symbolizing illumination, awakening, and multidimensional energy. The wheel radiates outward from this core, articulating a transformation hub and pointing to the conscious awareness that powers the rest of the mandala. The starburst motif in the background hints at the holographic principles behind the Holy Work of consciousness-raising. Each spoke of the wheel provides a download of higher intelligence, with each point supporting the others, as the movement between them becomes the dance of conscious evolution. Together, they form a field of higher intelligence, a frequency rich with the radiant sacred geometry of our potential awakening. The mandala is a fractal of insights to guide us on our transformation toward Homo luminosity.

Evolutionary eyes

These eyes see not just what is but what is becoming. They are attuned to higher perspectives, deeper insights, subtle truths, symbolic patterns, and emergent possibilities. Through them, we perceive the hidden wholeness beneath fragmentation; we see beyond the immediate into the potential. We begin to see as the soul sees, with spiritual vision. Evolutionary eyes develop once we accept the newly evolving paradigm mentioned throughout these pages. Everything we observe becomes a function of the process of becoming. All disasters, both man-made and natural, as well as all struggles, aches, and pains, begin to make sense as we understand that negativity comes to the surface for its purification and return to the natural order.

Evolutionary Trajectory

Throughout the entire cosmos, there is a forward-moving direction toward the north star of becoming. It is a trajectory that has been described as both an arrow[9] and an arc, leading and inviting the entire Universe to continue the ever-unfolding patterns of creation. This forward-moving thrust inspires humanity to transform and gives individuals a sense of direction for a positive future. This trajectory invites us to survive and thrive by becoming Homo luminous: radiant, coherent, and aligned with love, taking the journey from separation to unity.

John Lewis echoed the evolutionary trajectory with powerful clarity: "The arc of the moral universe is long, but it bends toward justice." But he also reminded us that it does not bend on its own; it bends because we rise to meet it. The moral arc of the universe bends because we get in "good trouble" and dare to pull that arc with our courage, our compassion, and our luminous becoming. Thus, evolution is not an accident but a process of participation. Barbara Marx Hubbard affirmed it is "evolution by choice, not by chance." Therefore, as cosmic citizens and co-creators, we are blessed with the opportunity

---

9 Phipps – see image on page 97

to help bend the arc toward unity, healing, and the birth of a more beautiful world.

Evolutionary impulse

The evolutionary impulse is a quickening! It is driven by the soul's sacred unrest to become more aligned with Source. The evolutionary impulse can be the subtle or overt energy that drives us to become more aware, compassionate, coherent, and cooperative. It is also the quiet urgency that whispers, "You were born for more." It is the fire behind your longing, the heartbeat of the cosmos thumping in your chest with the sacred rhythm of becoming.

Evolution is not something that happens to us; it is an infinite, ongoing miracle that unfolds through us. It is the spark of creation, which occurs in every infinitesimal moment, as something is continuously born out of nothing, again and again, in every infinitesimal now. The evolutionary impulse is the Divine whisper encoded in the spiral of our DNA, sparking the forward motion of the evolutionary trajectory, urging our souls to rise, expand, and remember.

Evolutionary worldview

The evolutionary worldview is the paradigm shift that is changing everything, reframing our understanding of life, our purpose, and humanity's role in the cosmos. It began replacing the deterministic and chaotic story of survival in the 1930s when futurists and emergentists first started singing songs of metamorphosis. The evolutionary worldview reveals that life is not a static state, but a dynamic, unfolding process. We are not here to fix the world but to evolve with it. Over the last eighty years, awareness has grown exponentially that consciousness and evolution are nearly synonymous, twin currents in the river of becoming. As humankind cultivates its evolutionary perspective, this expanded worldview is taking root in the collective unconscious, which Teilhard de Chardin referred to as the Noosphere—the thinking layer of the Earth itself.

Evolutionaries

Evolutionaries intuitively understand that 'we are the ones we have been waiting for.' Not as saviors but as co-creators, actively participating in the dance of co-creation. They feel the pulse of the future echoing in their bones, and they are driven to act with purpose, not to escape the world, but to help midwife its next expression, the Great Shift into the New Golden Age. Evolutionaries embody the upward spiral movement of evolution, embodying the changes, serving as catalysts, and carrying the frequency of what's next for humanity's uptick in consciousness. They are the individuals who accept that the transformation of our world depends on our faith in the future and our willingness to deliberately and consciously evolve ourselves. They are the teachers, healers, visionaries, spiritual pioneers, Lightworkers, Earthkeepers, and Starseeds committed to the thrival of our species, our planet, and the infinity of Universes.

Now, once again, let us take a deep breath and pick up our finely crafted, divinely inspired kaleidoscope. This time, we can call it a holographic kaleidoscope or a quantum kaleidoscope and imagine it is our window into evolution, not merely as science defines it, but as something more alive, more mystical. From a traditional scientific perspective, evolution is often described as a gradual process of biological adaptation. Through natural selection, genetic mutations that offer a survival advantage are passed on to future generations. Species evolve in response to environmental pressures, competition, and random change. Science views evolution as merely an impersonal, mechanistic dance of molecules directed by chance and necessity.

But what if there's more? What if we are not adrift in a chaotic cosmos, but we are riding a sacred spiral, guided by an unseen pattern, turning toward the light, and driven by the urge to become better and better? What if evolution is not only a process of adaptation but a revolution of becoming, inspired by an intelligent unfolding from within? What if each mutation, each leap forward, is not random but purposeful, nudged by an ancient force that knows precisely what it's doing?

To answer the above questions, scientists and visionaries began considering evolution as a matter of biology and a profound shift in consciousness. Since the 1930s, when the evolutionary worldview began to emerge, the seeds of a more profound understanding have been developing. The rigid scaffolding of Newtonian certainty began to dissolve as visionaries started listening to the deeper hum of the cosmos. The Jesuit paleontologist and mystic Pierre Teilhard de Chardin began the process with this famous quote: "We are not human beings having a spiritual experience; we are spiritual beings having a human experience."

Another turn of our magical kaleidoscope shows us that around this time, the world was reeling from two world wars, and the specter of nuclear annihilation cast a long shadow over humanity's psyche. Civilization stood on the edge of a precipice, haunted by the possibility that human ingenuity might outpace human wisdom. And yet, even amidst the rubble, rationing, and existential dread, the 1940s and 1950s witnessed a quiet yet profound flowering of consciousness.

While the world reeled from war and the looming specter of nuclear annihilation, subtle revolutions were taking place in living rooms, church basements, and healing circles. New Thought movements, whose roots stretched back a century to the healing insights of Phineas Quimby in the 1840s, began gaining momentum. Quimby taught that erroneous beliefs caused illness and could be healed through alignment with spiritual truth, a radical notion that gave birth to generations of metaphysical thinkers. From *Unity* to *Science of Mind*, these teachings emphasized mental causation, inner divinity, affirmative prayer, and the power of consciousness to shape reality. They offered comfort and a blueprint for human potential in a time of great uncertainty. Around this time, early systems theorists began mapping the elegant complexity of life, suggesting that everything from cells to societies and ecosystems was interrelated. The first whispers of ecological awareness began to stir, hinting that the Earth was not a resource to be conquered but a living being to be honored.

Turning our kaleidoscope to today, we find ourselves at an eerily similar inflection point. While world wars no longer shadow us in the same way, we are plagued by a more subtle and dispersed kind of apocalyptic anxiety as we witness the unraveling of institutions, climate collapse, mass extinctions, digital isolation, spiritual disorientation, the erosion of truth, the degradation of lawful order and civic trust, and the rise of global authoritarianism. These entangled crises infiltrate society's structures and the architecture of the human psyche. These fears are diffuse, atomized, and woven into the very fabric of modern life.

However, another flowering is occurring amidst this darkness that parallels the 1940s uptick in consciousness. Another renaissance of consciousness is underway. Words like trauma, nervous system regulation, and shadow integration have entered the mainstream lexicon. Yoga, meditation, plant medicine, energy medicine, energy healing, energy psychology, and evolutionary psychology are no longer fringe or woo-woo; they create and provide tools for an awakening humanity. We are witnessing the rise of an interconnected, empathic, soul-literate, evolutionary worldview. This worldview honors not just what we know but *how* we know. Many integrated psychological theoretical frameworks, such as CP, have emerged within this metamorphic field. They are luminous frameworks that bridge the psychological and spiritual, the ancient and the quantum. CP recognizes that what we often call symptoms may be signals of soul initiation, or *"Dark Nights of the Soul,"* as *Thomas Moore, Ph.D., refers to* them. These frameworks are responding to the moment, teaching that the human psyche is not broken but birthing something more expansive, contributing to the uptick in consciousness necessary for our thrival.

In *Celestial Psychology*® (CP), we further develop this lineage, expanding it beyond the personal into the planetary, where healing the *psyche* becomes inseparable from healing the world, and awakening is not just a private event but a universal evolutionary imperative. Our sacred soul-searching kaleidoscope reveals the soul of humanity pressing outward, spiraling upward, yearning to become whole, luminous, and more in alignment with the heart of the cosmos. We no longer view evolution as a cold and accidental mechanism, but as a living, invitational call to participate. Evolution becomes a revolution we are meant to embody. Not with violence but with vision. Not with resistance but with resonance. Not by dominating nature or humanity, but by remembering that we are part of nature and humankind is naturally evolving.

The evolution of consciousness is the revolution written in the language of Light encoded in our cells. As more of us awaken to our luminous inheritance, Light Language is emerging as a form of expression not bound by grammar or translation but by vibration itself. This multidimensional mode of communication bypasses the mind and speaks directly to the soul, transmitting frequencies of remembrance, healing, and activation. It is the music of becoming, the resonance of our return, the sound of the stars within us learning to speak again. The evolution of consciousness is written in the DNA of stars twinkling in our bones, whispering, "*You were made for this becoming.*"

Thus, when we allow ourselves to see and experience evolution not merely as a series of physical or historical changes in form, but as a living, breathing process of transformation that operates on multiple levels—biological, psychological, energetic, political, economic, and spiritual — we become inspired. We begin to sense that evolution does not happen to us but through us. It becomes a conscious revolution of being, inviting us to participate fully in remaking ourselves and our world.

When viewed through the metaphoric lens of our kaleidoscope, the ever-shifting patterns of evolution continue to reveal more than mere adaptation. The emerging images inspire awe, evoke wonder, and stir a subtle yet powerful and revolutionary expansion of consciousness that feels nothing short of exhilarating. These patterns trace the upward spiral, a dancing sacred geometry of becoming better and better, always pointing toward greater coherence, beauty, and possibility. The evolutionary impulse fuels this spiral; it is an intelligent current urging us to move beyond survival to thrival. Evolution is no longer solely about the survival of the fittest but about the flourishing of the most awakened. Those who collaborate, cultivate compassion, and choose to love boldly and live consciously are and ever will be the ones leading this next great turning of the spiral.

The Twelve Codes of the Evolutionary Trajectory

And in that spiral, we rise, not as lone warriors, but as a symphony of souls remembering how to move as one. Each act of awakening, each choice to love, and each whisper of healing adds to the music of this revolution. We are not climbing alone; we are co-ascending, carried by the momentum of all who dare to dream, evolve, and embody the luminous truth of who we truly are.

The recent rise (pun fully intended) of the word *thrival* is further evidence of our awakening. It marks a quantum leap from survival consciousness to a paradigm rooted in abundance, purpose, and full-spectrum aliveness. One need only skim the curriculum of modern coaching programs, wellness programs, personal development paths, psychotherapeutic models, or social justice movements to see the signs: the new goal is thriving, thriving physically, mentally, emotionally, spiritually, socially, and financially.

This shift—from survival to thrival—invites us to reimagine evolution. What if evolution is about what changes, and who recognizes those changes? What if the great unfolding is not just happening to life but *through* it and *for* it? These questions suggest that evolution is no longer merely a physical process but the sacred unfolding of consciousness. Evolution becomes a God-like creative unfolding, an invitation to awaken, align, embody, and become new ways of being, giving birth to infinite possibilities.

And perhaps most radically: what if an uplift in awareness is not just a fortunate side-effect of evolution but its very purpose? After all, what is evolution, if not the ongoing revelation of consciousness into ever more complex, compassionate, and creative forms? Life is not merely surviving. Life is striving to know itself, to awaken, to become. And we mere mortals have the blessed opportunity to participate in this supernatural process.

EVOLUTIONARY AFFIRMATIONS

Evolutionary Eyes
"I see with evolutionary eyes—attuned to the hidden beauty of becoming, awakened to the deeper patterns unfolding through time."

"My vision pierces illusion; I witness the sacred architecture of transformation in all things."

Evolutionary Trajectory
"I trust the arc of my evolutionary trajectory, knowing it bends toward coherence, cooperation, compassion, community, justice, and grace."

"Each step I take is aligned with the soul's blueprint, drawing me toward my luminous potential."

Evolutionary Impulse
"I honor the evolutionary impulse rising within me—the sacred push toward expansion, wholeness, and awakened embodiment."

"The fire of evolution fuels my becoming; I move forward not out of fear but from the joy of unfolding."

Evolutionary Worldview
"I hold an evolutionary worldview that sees challenge as invitation, and chaos as the womb of renewal."

"I perceive the world as a living organism, evolving through love, wisdom, and conscious participation."

Evolutionaries (as an identity)
"I am an evolutionary—one who dares to dream, disrupt, and devote myself to the future flowering of humanity."

"As an evolutionary, I walk in alignment with soul, source, and the spiral of becoming.

CHAPTER TWO
THE TWELVE CODES OF THE EVOLUTIONARY TRAJECTORY

Activating Consciousness. Anchoring Light. Becoming Luminous.

As we examine this sacred unfolding more closely, we find specific recurring forces emerging and shaping our evolutionary path—forces I refer to as the evolutionary virtues or the Codes of the Evolutionary Trajectory. These twelve guiding energies are not merely philosophical ideals; they are living frequencies, vibrational signatures that shape our consciousness, sculpt our becoming, and illuminate the path of emergence into Homo-luminous beings.

Some arise as foundational pulses, such as the Code of Change, the Code of Continuity, and the Code of Competition. These are not mere biological mechanisms but archetypal forces encoded into the very blueprint of life. Change is the catalytic spark, always urging us beyond the comfort of old identities. Continuity is the sacred thread that anchors our becoming within an unbroken lineage of life, soul, and starlight. Competition, at its highest frequency, sharpens discernment and awakens adaptive brilliance—not through conquest but through dynamic refinement.

Others form a higher-frequency navigation system: the Code of Commitment, the Code of Coherence, the Code of Congruency, and the Code of Complexity. These help stabilize and fine-tune our interior alignment with the greater evolutionary field. They call us into deeper integrity, inner harmony, multidimensional perception, and sustained devotion to the sacred path of becoming.

The other codes speak to this journey's relational and collective harmonics: the Code of Creativity, the Code of Compassion, the Code of Cooperation, and the Code of Community. These emergent virtues reflect the flowering of the heart and the birth of collaborative consciousness. They remind us that evolution is not a solitary ascent but a shared dance of expression, empathy, synergy, and belonging.

Communication is the twelfth 'C', the carrier wave that runs through all the other codes of the Evolutionary Trajectory. Compassion without expression remains merely potential; cooperation depends on mutual understanding; coherence requires shared signals; even competition can evolve into refinement when mediated with caring and respectful communication.

Together, these Codes do not merely describe evolution—they transmit it. They activate the crystalline structures of our light bodies, attune us to unity consciousness, and prepare us to become Supraconscious Creators of a luminous, multidimensional reality.

1. The Code of Change

Change is the catalyst of evolution.

The Code of Change catalyzes evolution. The ever-present force that nudges, disrupts, and invites us beyond our previous forms. It is the pulse of becoming that is encoded in every cell, star, and system. Change does not ask permission; it arrives like a cosmic tide, dissolving what no longer serves and awakening what longs to emerge. In CP, we recognize change not as chaos but as choreography—the divine dance of entropy and emergence through which life reshapes itself. To resist change is to stagnate; to embrace it is to participate consciously in the unfolding mystery of transformation.

2. The Code of Continuity

Continuity is the sacred thread that binds us across lifetimes, timelines, and ancestral knowing.

The Code of Continuity is the invisible thread that weaves through all becoming. While change stirs the waters of transformation, continuity holds the memory of wholeness. It is the deep current beneath the surface waves—the lineage of light that connects past, present, and future. In the framework of CP, continuity is not mere repetition; it is the sacred echo of the original intention, the resonance of the soul across lifetimes and dimensions. It reminds us that evolution is not abandonment—it is remembrance. To honor continuity is to root in the wisdom of what endures while reaching toward the luminous unknown

3. The Code of Competition

Competition is the refining edge that calls forth discernment, strength, and adaptive brilliance.

Competition is not about domination but discernment, refinement, and the evolutionary brilliance that emerges through contrast. In its highest octave, competition sharpens our gifts, challenges our assumptions, and awakens latent potential. It invites us to rise, not at the expense of others but in resonance with our excellence. In CP, competition is viewed as a sacred tension that catalyzes growth, a vibrational pressure that reveals the edges of our becoming. When freed from egoic distortion, competition becomes an invitation to align more fully with our soul's radiance and respond with grace to life's call to step forward

4. The Code of Commitment

The stabilizing vow to keep showing up for the journey, devoted, grounded, and aligned.

Commitment roots us, provides the backbone, and inspires the sacred devotion required for true transformation. Commitment is the frequency of follow-through, the anchor that holds us steady through waves of change. Not rooted in duty, but in soul-allegiance, commitment is the act of showing up repeatedly—for our healing, becoming, and the future we are co-creating. Commitment drives service to others with the sacred devotion required for true transformation; it is the frequency of follow-through and anchors us steadily through waves of change. It is the spiritual discipline of not turning away or engaging in spiritual bypassing when the going gets tough, or when cognitive dissonance threatens to fracture our psyches.

5. The Code of Coherence

When we are in alignment, when our systems are harmonized, we become the signal for the Divine greater field.

Coherency is the inner alignment that allows all aspects of a system—or a self—to move in harmony. It is clarity within complexity, a sacred synergy that reveals itself when energy flows without distortion. In cosmic or biological systems, coherence stabilizes the Field and supports evolution. In our personal lives, it is the experience of being in a state of flow, when life seems to move with us, not against us.

In these states of alignment, we often encounter synchronicity—those meaningful coincidences that feel like cosmic winks, gentle affirmations that we are on the right path. Synchronicity arises when the inner and outer worlds reflect one another with uncanny precision. It is a sacred signpost of coherence in action, an energetic affirmation that we are attuned to the Universe's rhythm.

6. The Code of Congruency

Authenticity is alignment made visible.

Psychologically, congruency is the alignment between our internal experience and our external expression. It is the felt sense of integrity—when our thoughts, emotions, beliefs, and behaviors are in authentic resonance with one another. We move through life with clarity, confidence, and inner peace when we are in alignment with our values.

Incongruence, by contrast, creates inner conflict. We may feel fragmented, unsure, or misaligned with our words or actions. This psychic friction disrupts our flow and can lead to dis-ease in body, mind, and spirit. The Code of Congruency tells us that evolution is a deeply personal process. It teaches us to live from the inside out—to speak, act, and create from the core of who we truly are. When we embody congruency, we feel whole and become a source of congruency for the world around us.

7. The Code of Complexity

The elegance of life is revealed through its intricacy.

Complexity arises as life becomes increasingly intricate, layered, and intelligent. From single-celled organisms to symphonic ecosystems, from tribal myths to quantum models of reality, evolution naturally builds toward greater nuance and depth. Complexity doesn't imply chaos—it reflects the sacred geometry of wholeness. This Code teaches us to hold multiplicity without fragmentation and to honor diversity as a pathway to harmony. It creates elegance out of integration, harmonizing infinite parts into a whole. It is the art of the cosmos refining itself into conscious form.

8. The Code of Creativity

Creativity is the holy impulse to imagine, innovate, and provide a path for the Universe to know itself through form.

The Code of Creativity is the divine spark that bridges the unseen and the manifest, turning vision into structure and insight into embodiment. Creativity is not a luxury for the inspired few; it is the evolutionary force that transforms frequency into function, soul into symbol, and light into language. In CP, creativity is the sacred engine of becoming, empowering us to compose new realities, respond to change with grace, and give shape to the ineffable. We do not merely express through creativity—we *participate* in the unfolding design of a more luminous world.

As the Universe sparked itself in the beginning, perhaps creativity was more a frequency than a word. If so, it would have been a vibration so pure, so concentrated with possibility, that it ruptured silence and birthed space, time, and light in a single, ineffable spark. Perhaps the Big Bang was not merely an explosion, but a divine exhalation, a cosmic yes, a moment when the unmanifest dared to become visible. It was the Universe dreaming itself into form through the ecstasy of expansion. That spark still pulses within us—a seed of brilliance encoded in our cells, stars, and stories. To create is to touch that origin point, to remember that we, too, are fragments of that first fire, made not just of matter but of meaning, consciousness, and spirit.

9. The Code of Compassion

Compassion is the heart frequency that dissolves the illusion of separation, reminding us that lifting others is lifting the whole.

Compassion is the ultimate heart-opener and a sign of advanced consciousness. It softens judgment, releases fear, and restores connection. The Code of Compassion, in evolutionary terms, is not just an emotional state or a moral virtue but a neurological and energetic advancement. The more we expand our consciousness with meditation and personal growth practices, the more empathy we develop and the more we feel with and for others. We become better equipped to care for ourselves and others equally because we no longer buy the illusion that we are separate from the "others."

This Code invites us to move from survival to soulfulness. In recovery, the shift from "What's in it for me?" to "How can I serve?" is not just behavioral—it's vibrational. Compassion signals that the heart has been reawakened and the ego has softened enough to allow empathy to take the lead. This evolutionary current turns pain into purpose, allowing the wounded healer to become a luminous guide.

Compassion activates unity, and unity is the key that accelerates the entire Ascension spiral. We recognize that we are One with the Universe and One with everything in it. By dissolving the illusion of separation, the number one trick of the Egoic Mind that Eckhart Tolle and ACIM teach. When we release the grip of fear and anxiety and replace these negative emotions with love for one another and the entire Universe, with this Code, we become love in action; we facilitate the collective awakening and heal the whole human story.

10. The Code of Cooperation

Life thrives through connection, not separation.

Cooperation marks the evolutionary shift from rivalry to resonance and competition to synergy. It represents the movement from survival of the fittest to thrival of the most collaborative. Thrival is a hallmark of conscious evolution—life no longer adapts merely to exist but awakens to connect and flourish. While early evolution models emphasized competition, nature, through the Code of Cooperation, repeatedly demonstrates that the most enduring systems are those founded on mutual beneficence, shared intention, and interdependence. Cells cooperate to form organs; species coexist to balance ecosystems; and humans evolve faster when we share, support, and uplift one another. Cooperation is the soul's strategy for sustainability—and in the context of the Ascension process, it becomes the energetic blueprint for collective awakening. Through conscious cooperation, we activate the gridwork of unity consciousness, allowing humanity to rise to higher dimensions together rather than fracture apart.

11. The Code of Community

We rise in collective circles, not in silos.

Community is where all the other Codes converge. It is both the container and the catalyst for conscious evolution. Community is a vital and often under-acknowledged factor in evolutionary progress.

Whether we are speaking of cellular communities forming tissues and organs or human beings forming heart-centered collectives, societies, or soul circles, it is in relationships that new forms emerge. The Code of Community teaches that no soul evolves in isolation. We evolve together. We are wired to co-create. Just as early human survival depended on tribal cooperation, today's leap in consciousness depends on our ability to awaken as a collective. We cannot rise alone; we will not ascend alone. No species survives in isolation, and no soul evolves alone. The Code of Community enables the sharing of wisdom, the reflection of growth, and the amplification of love. Whether formed through bloodlines, soul contracts, or shared visions, communities are the sacred ecosystems in which individual transformation takes root and multiplies. Heaven finds form on Earth, built on reciprocal nourishment and service with the Code of Community.

12. The Code of Communication

Communication is the thread- the communion of the evolutionary trajectory.

Communication is the sacred thread that weaves the entire tapestry of evolution. From chemical signaling in single-celled organisms to human language, music, prayer, and telepathy, communication is how life shares information, adapts, and evolves. It is not only the bridge between beings—it is the *field* through which consciousness transmits itself. In the journey toward Homo-luminous, communication becomes vibrational, energetic, and multidimensional. It fine-tunes our capacity for intuition, empathy, resonance, and nonverbal knowing.

In this view, the evolutionary process reveals itself as a mechanism of natural law and a conscious, sacred unfolding. It is life reaching for more life, the Universe seeking more knowing—through connection, creativity, and the profound remembering of who and what we truly are: spiritual beings having a human experience.

The Codes of the Evolutionary Trajectory are not abstract ideals but invitations to embody this truth. We learn to hold paradox and possibility with grace when we attune to the Code of Complexity. When we embody the Code of Cooperation, we shift from competition to co-creation. The Code of Coherency brings us into inner alignment, while the Code of Congruency calls us into authentic wholeness. The Code of Compassion opens the heart as an evolutionary organ of light, and the Code of Community reminds us that we rise together.

These codes are not imposed from above; they are encoded within us, deep within our DNA, and are waiting to be activated. They are the soul's instructions, also referred to as the 'imaginal cells' for the shift from Homo sapiens to Homo luminous, from unconscious survival to conscious, multidimensional thrival. As we awaken to them, we become witnesses to the evolutionary process and willing, radiant participants in its unfolding.

AFFIRMATIONS FOR THE SACRED CODES

"I am a conscious participant in the sacred unfolding of life.
The 12 Sacred Codes of the Evolutionary Trajectory live within me.
I honor their wisdom. I activate their frequencies.
Through my awareness, I evolve.
Through my love, I align.
Through my presence, I remember who I truly am."

INVOCATION TO THE EVOLUTIONARY FIELD

"Beloved Source of all becoming,
Ancient Intelligence woven through time and stardust,
I open my heart to the sacred spiralling codes of evolution.
Let the Code of Change catalyze my willingness to BEcome.
Let the Code of Continuity thread my awareness across all timelines and lifetimes.
Let the Code of Competition refine my adaptive brilliance.
Let the Code of Commitment stabilize my vow to show up and persevere.
Let the Code of Coherence align my inner and outer worlds.
Let the Code of Congruency enlighten my every thought, word, and deed.
Let the Code of Complexity open my multidimensional perception.
Let the Code of Creativity spark my innovativeness to make the invisible visible.
Let the Code of Compassion soften my resistance.
Let the Code of Cooperation guide my relationships.
Let the Code of Community root me in soul-centered belonging.
May I remember that I am not separate from the Universe—
I am the Universe, becoming conscious of itself.
I invoke the path of luminous becoming.
Let me walk it with grace, courage, and joy.
So it is, and so I rise."

CHAPTER THREE
WE ARE THOSE FISH!

Peering through the viewing end of our finely crafted evolutionary meta-kaleidoscope, we catch a glimpse of the origins of life. The chamber is alive with movement, shimmering pulses of light and color swirling through the darkness like sparks of divine intention. Tiny globes of possibility float and flicker, suspended in a primal sea. We watch as simple, single-celled organisms emerge—vibrating with potential, splitting and multiplying in rhythm with a pulse older than time itself. These microscopic miracles drift and cluster, forming fragile membranes that exchange signals and evolve in a slow, sacred dance.

Turning the future visioning kaleidoscope's tube once more, we leap forward through vast corridors of time. The patterns shift into glistening scales and sinuous movement as an underwater kingdom comes alive before our eyes. We behold the great age of fish, those ancient navigators of liquid worlds who ruled the seas, lakes, and rivers for nearly fifty million years. They glide in schools like living constellations, their sleek bodies reflecting the primordial light of Earth's watery womb. We recognize they are the basis for all life, for all life originates in water. We hail the early philosophers who recognized that their proliferation symbolized the *life germ* itself.[iv]

The scene flickers and changes with another slight rotation of our magical kaleidoscope. The oceans are draining away, and the once-graceful, prolific fish are now floundering in muddy pools of primordial soup, flopping and gasping for air at the edge of extinction. Riverbeds are drying around them like closing doors. Their gills strain for breath, and their bodies twitch instinctively, aching with the need for adaptation. In this liminal moment, caught between water and land, past and possibility, they embody the raw tension of evolution.

They are not merely surviving; they are *becoming*.

Hoping to see something more pleasant, we turn the kaleidoscope's tube slightly once more, and the image shifts again. We are thrilled to witness a miraculous transformation. Once confined to the sea, the fish have grown limbs strong enough to bear their weight, backbones to support their new mobility, and rudimentary lungs to draw breath from the air. They rise from the muddy pools like pioneers of possibility, crawling toward an unfamiliar world. Their bodies speak of courage written in the Codes of the Evolutionary Trajectory. They face the ancient proverbial decision etched into DNA: *adapt, perish, evolve, or disappear.*

And then, with a soft click of time's lens, we set our magical kaleidoscope to the present.

Suddenly, we realize that this image—the fish flailing in a drying pool of primordial mud, its gills yearning for breath, its scales beginning to shimmer into feathers—is not merely a chapter in natural history. It has become an evolutionary archetype—a living symbol embedded deep within our collective psyche. It reflects a primal threshold moment: the tension between extinction and transformation, the ache of adaptation, the evolutionary squeeze between what was and what could be.

This archetype urgently speaks to us now, in the epoch of The Great Shift, because we are teetering on the edge of *what is known* and what lies beyond *the unknown next*. The archetype of the fish gasping in the primordial mud holds the memory of every species, every soul, that has ever reached for the impossible, through pain, through pressure, through perseverance. It is the image of life insisting on itself, even when the environment can no longer support the old form. It is the signature moment when the necessity to evolve becomes encoded in the body, the mind, and the spirit.

We are those fish struggling in primordial mud!

We are gasping for survival on a planet that is gasping for its survival as well. The waters of our comfort zones are boiling and receding. The riverbeds of outdated ecological, economic, political, and emotional systems are cracking wide open. The scaffolding of the familiar is disintegrating, and we are called to either evolve or go extinct. This archetypal moment is not just biological; it is spiritual, psychological, and existential. We are being asked to breathe in new ways, to grow etheric limbs, crystalline third eyes, and new layers of light bodies that we never knew we had. We are also being asked and prompted to risk stepping out of the known and onto a strange, unsteady shore of infinite multidimensional consciousness.

We are being challenged beyond imagination in our beliefs, relationships, health, spiritual identities, and collective agreements. And yet, just as those ancient fish carried within them the hidden blueprint for amphibians and birds, we carry within us the codes for the luminous human! The archetype of the fish struggling in the mud is not a symbol of failure. It is the sacred blueprint of transformation.

"No mud, no lotus."

This beautiful metaphor and famous quote by the beloved Vietnamese Zen Master, Thich Nhat Hanh, is the perfect reminder that suffering is not separate from joy or enlightenment. The lotus, a symbol of purity and awakening, only grows from the depths of muddy water. As we turn our kaleidoscope for becoming, let us embrace our suffering, not avoid it, as suffering provides fertile ground from which wisdom, compassion, and transformation arise. However, embracing suffering is not the same as glorifying or rooting for it. Awakening does not require devastation to bloom, just as the lotus blooms without destroying the pond.

This sacred blueprint of transformation lives within each of us. It is not reserved for saints, mystics, or mythic heroes. Just as the lotus requires the mud to bloom and the fish requires friction to grow wings, our current struggles are not signs of failure but signals of becoming. The discomfort, disorientation, and yearning for something more are evolutionary stirrings. They indicate that something within us is being recalibrated, reshaped, and reborn. We are not simply breaking down; we are being broken *open*. The sacred blueprint does not guarantee ease, but it does promise a sense of meaning. And when we recognize that our pain is not punishment but preparation, we begin to see the mud not as a mess, but as the fertile ground from which our luminous selves can rise.

As visionary Barbara Marx Hubbard reminds us, evolution rarely announces itself with fanfare. Most of the time, it unfolds in quiet urgency. "We are at a critical evolutionary event [like the one when fish evolved]," she writes, "that surely went unnoticed by the adventurous fish and his friends. Similarly, the human family has not yet understood the significance of present events. We are still lacing a perspective broad enough to see what's happening."

And so—as we dare to attempt to lace a perspective broad enough to see what's [truly] happening and when we dare to deeply look again into the sacred, cosmic kaleidoscope for becoming with our newly developing evolutionary eyes—*we can begin to see the signs of a glorious future.*

CHAPTER FOUR
WE ARE THOSE DUDES!

To see what is happening today, we make another turn of this visionary kaleidoscope, looking again at the past. This time, the chambers reflect images of primitive man. We see a multitude of different species struggling to survive, competing, fighting, and killing each other. One species survives—*Homo sapiens* (wise man). At first glance, it appeared that this being survived because he was the fittest; yet, a closer look reveals that survival had more to do with how he earned his name.

Generally, wisdom or awareness cannot be seen; it can only be known by what becomes evident from it. In this case, the arrival of wisdom is apparent in the actions of this particular species of the genus Homo, which contributed to their survival. *Homo sapiens* survived by forming tribes based on cooperation and regeneration. They protected and provided for each other by creating safe places to grow and thrive. This ability shows that primitive man grew wiser by banding together in groups (like cells surviving in living organisms) to share their knowledge. Sharing their wisdom helped them develop sufficient cooperation, empathy, and compassion, which has brought us to where we are today.

The arrival of awareness, however, is underplayed by Darwinians and evolutionary psychologists, whose kaleidoscope reveals a different story. Through their lens, primitive man is merely biologically adapting. Evolutionary psychology, a branch of science dedicated to understanding human adaptations and neurobiological functions, tends to frame the brain as a computational organ, with chemistry and physics as its software. These scientists are, admittedly, "relentlessly past-oriented"[v] and often fail to consider that our neural circuits are not just relics of survival strategies gone by but are actively being redesigned to meet the emergent challenges of this moment.

Most crucially, they discount the impact of consciousness itself- the wild card of all wild cards. They overlook the mystery that awareness changes biology. That compassion reshapes circuitry. That insight can rewire lifetimes and even heal ancestral trauma.

Turning our evolutionary kaleidoscope to today, we discover the Field of epigenetics, hailed as the *new biology*. According to cell biologist Bruce H. Lipton, Ph.D., epigenetics is the "Control above the genes… and the cell's operations are primarily molded by its interaction with the environment, not by its genetic code." He contends that in this new biology, the brain and all the "mem-brains" of our cells are the hardware, while consciousness is the software. [vi] Lipton's anthropomorphic correlation[vii] between consciousness and cellular structure suggests that the human brain and body are the hardware programmable by the software of awareness, intention, and beliefs.

Nearly a century after the pioneers of the New Thought Movement proposed that, when deliberately directed, consciousness or thoughts can heal disease, science is now catching up. Lipton's research offers compelling scientific evidence that cells respond to our thoughts and perceptions. As we each incorporate these powerful truths individually, we contribute to the rise in humanity's collective consciousness. As a species, we are learning, much like the Hundredth Monkey Phenomenon has shown us, that the ripple effect produces a new kind of human. We are learning to rewrite our limiting and false beliefs; for instance, 'we are doomed to whatever our genes have dictated.' We are discovering that we are not at the mercy of our biology, and we can and must become active participants in our development, also known as our becoming. We are unleashing the long-dormant power of consciousness, bringing energy, light, and information to matter and becoming capable of making miracles.

Our genes are not our destiny. Orison Swett Marden, an American spiritual visionary of the New Thought Movement, once declared,

> **"Our destiny changes with our thoughts; we shall become what we wish to become, do what we wish to do, when our habitual thoughts correspond with our desires."**

Marden would undoubtedly approve of the New Biology and consciousness studies if he were alive today. He might even revise his quote to resonate with epigenetics and the emerging awareness that our biology is not a fixed script but a living, evolving symphony of choices and conditions. Perhaps his rewrite would be,

> **"My genetic predisposition is only the recipe; I am the cook, and high-level wellness is my delicious dish!"**

Yes, we are the cooks. But we are also the ones sourcing the ingredients. And what are those ingredients? They are the subtle and not-so-subtle energies we allow into our fields—thoughts, emotions, relationships, environments, foods, and frequencies. Every choice, conscious or unconscious, adds to the mixture. Our lives are not just made of matter; they are infused with meaning, and meaning is a vibrational phenomenon. Genes may write the first draft, but we are the editors, the chefs, and the quantum conductors of our own becoming.

No longer can we blame the cookbook—or the lineage from which it came. Our Quality of Life (QOL) is shaped not merely by circumstance, but by the quantity of the ingredients of light, energy, and information we allow, embody, and integrate. It is further multiplied by the Quality and Quantity of energy, frequency, and vibration that gel and become harmonious or coherent in our subtle energy field.

$$\wedge \text{ QOL } \alpha \wedge \text{ QOLEI} \times \text{QQ-CEFV}$$

We will explore this updated formula throughout these pages as it offers a new paradigm for thriving in alignment with evolutionary consciousness, coherence, and revolutionary choices.

When we last peered into our evolutionary kaleidoscope, we saw the surviving prehistoric being evolve into more intelligent, more cooperative, and increasingly compassionate *Homo sapiens*. And now, with a slight turn of the kaleidoscope to today, we discover the shocking, humbling, and oddly hilarious truth: **we are still those dudes**, those prehistoric dudes continuing the journey of the evolving *Homo sapiens*. Despite our smartphones, space programs, and spiritual workshops, we remain works-in-progress—cave dwellers of consciousness, banging rocks (crystals) together in the dark, trying to spark light. We carry within us the same ancient fears, the same tribal wiring, and the same deep longing to belong and survive.

Our brains still house the ancient circuitry of survival, known as the reptilian or mammalian brain, and, in more popular vernacular, it is also referred to as 'the monkey mind,' derived from Buddhist teachings. This portion of the brain is responsible for our most primitive, reactive, and unconscious behaviors, as well as our ever-vigilant, reactive, and wired-for-fight, flight, freeze, or fawn responses to situations. It served our ancestors well in the wild, but in today's world of emotional complexity and spiritual awakening, it often short-circuits our higher aspirations.

Thankfully, layered above the older survival system is the neocortex—specifically the prefrontal cortex, which author Michael Dowd[10] has affectionately termed the Higher Porpoise because of its shape and 'purpose.' Scientists consider it the most recent evolutionary upgrade in the human brain. This region governs empathy, foresight, reflection, and moral reasoning. It is cultivated through practices such as meditation, visualization, and intentional focus. Though anatomically distinct from the pineal gland, the prefrontal cortex is deeply synergistic with the intuitive functions of the third eye. Together, they form a kind of inner observatory—where vision meets wisdom. The prefrontal cortex

---

[10] *Thank God for Evolution*

allows us to ease or override our reptilian impulses and monkey-mind chatter. It is the neurological seat of conscious evolution, where intention begins to override instinct, reactivity gives way to response, and we begin to glimpse what it truly means to become human by design.

The Third Eye, known as the Ajna chakra, has long been revered in ancient traditions as the gateway to inner vision. It is associated with the pineal gland, a tiny, light-sensitive structure nestled deep within the brain. Though no larger than a grain of rice, the pineal gland holds outsized mythic significance. Descartes called it the 'seat of the soul.' In other metaphysical systems, it is seen as the crystal lens through which we perceive subtle truths and spiritual realities. The pineal regulates circadian rhythms through melatonin production, but its esoteric function may be even more profound: attuning us to the rhythms of higher consciousness. When activated through meditation, breathwork, or states of deep coherence, the pineal acts like a bio-spiritual antenna—receiving impressions from beyond the veil, a sacred transmitter of light, energy, and information, a living relic of our multidimensional design

So, thankfully, something new is stirring. We are entering a phase of evolution shaped not by tooth and claw but by intention, insight, and soul-level adaptation. We are becoming aware of ourselves as light beings with auric layers of energy that can be harnessed, refined, directed, and expanded for healing and transformation. We are learning to evolve consciously, not just in body or brain, but in vibration, energy, and light. Thus, conscious evolution invites us to engage in practices that involve subtle energy manipulation, enhanced perception, emotional mastery, and energetic coherence.

We are learning—sometimes slowly and sometimes painfully—that the physical, mental, and spiritual sensations we experience and the realities we manifest are not random. They are shaped by a deeper Law of Responsiveness, a fundamental truth in physics and metaphysics: that the Universe and all its systems do not function on random chaos but on reciprocal dynamics. The Law of Responsiveness assumes a more profound meaning when applied to the evolutionary kaleidoscope throughout the pages of this book. We recognize that consciousness is not a passive bystander but an active participant in the creation process. Spiritual teachers such as Dr. Joe Dispenza drill it into our heads, "what we attend to, we amplify." And Michael Beckwith rose to fame with his adage, "Energy flows where attention goes." As we practice our manifestation visualizations with Mike Dooley, we are continually reminded "what we allow in shapes what we put out."

The Law of Responsiveness suggests that every human being is a tuning instrument. The more refined our inner receptivity becomes, and the more willing we are to receive light, energy, and information, the more coherent the frequency and vibration of our actions, emotions, and creations become. Our nervous system, subtle energy bodies, and even our cellular biology are constantly in dialogue with the stimuli of existence.

This deeper Law teaches us that evolution is not about control but receptivity, discernment, and intelligent participation. It reminds us that our quality of life is not a matter of fate but of frequency. We are capable of evolving into a higher level of awareness. Our receptor capacities, i.e., our ability to sense, filter, and integrate high-frequency stimuli, are directly proportional to our action capacities, i.e., our ability to create, respond, and affect the world with clarity and power.

In other words, the more stimulus, Light, Energy, and Information (LEI) we consciously choose to receive, metabolize, and harmonize with coherent energy, frequency, and vibration, the more empowered, luminous, and aligned our embodiment becomes.

This relationship is expressed through the symbol for direct proportion "α" in the upgraded formula:

$$\wedge QOL \; \alpha \; \wedge QOLEI \times QQ\text{-}CEFV$$

Quality of Life **increases in direct proportion to the** Quantity of Light, Energy, and Information **we allow into our field, multiplied by the quality and quantity of** Coherence **we cultivate within our** Energetic **field of** Frequency **and** Vibration.

This equation echoes Einstein's assertion: "The higher the frequency of the light, the more energy…" In this context, Homo sapiens become Homo luminous, enhancing their quality of life in direct proportion to the amount of light-energy-information they embody, align with, and radiate as spiritual beings in human form.

We are spiritual beings inhabiting physical bodies encoded for an upgrade of infinitely increasing cooperation, empathy, and compassion. Coming to terms with the profound responsibility we each have as co-creators of our reality, and, therefore, the collective reality, is a tremendous leap—a quantum leap forward. Whether or not we accept the entire Homo-luminous being/evolutionary process package, we are still responsible for the choices we make regarding the quantity-of-light-energy-information (QOLEI) we bring into ourselves, and the subsequent quality-of-life (QOL) we create.

The path of transformation, while sometimes joyous and revelatory, is not always easy. It requires consistent effort, attention, and willingness. But it is worth it. The intensity of the effort we make to bring light, energy, and information into the membranes of our etheric, physical, and cellular bodies produces changes that are, quite literally, life-changing. The upward, forward movement of evolution naturally intensifies across all dimensions of life—health, finances, relationships, and purpose. We learn how to evolve consciously, deliberately, and luminously when practicing state-of-the-art consciousness-raising activities.

Science is sounding the call to survive and truly thrive; we must evolve together. This means integrating the wisdom of energy medicine, the promises of epigenetics, and the liberating truths of the biology of belief. It means embracing the revelatory landscapes of quantum physics, the insightful depths of evolutionary psychology, and the transformative power of consciousness studies. We must transcend Darwin's purely physical paradigm, for we now understand evolution is not only shaped by biology – it is sculpted by consciousness itself.

And as we awaken to this astonishing reality, something extraordinary begins to dawn within us:

We realize we are not passive passengers on the evolutionary ride, but we are becoming conscious co-creators within the Quantum Field itself. Our thoughts, once considered fleeting and intangible, are now recognized as vibrational directives—energizing patterns that shape probabilities and influence everything from the crystallization of snowflakes to the orchestration of distant quasars. We are no longer just stargazers; we are phasing the cosmos into coherence, harmonizing with what ancient mystics called Father Universe and Mother Earth.

We are creating beings—deliberate, luminous architects of a new epoch. With awakened minds and hearts, we are co-designing new societies, reimagining our neuro-architecture, rewriting our psychobiology, and reweaving timelines that align with love, justice, and evolutionary grace. Co-creation is not fantasy; it is the flowering of our species' next chapter. And we are writing this next great chapter together, with every choice, every frequency, every breath of becoming.

Neuroscientist Bruce Lipton echoes the above paragraphs and knows emphatically that the human brain is preparing for a quantum leap. Evolutionary theorist Michael Cotton believes we can hack evolution through higher brain activation. Undoubtedly, we are establishing new neural pathways and exploring the architectural blueprints of the mind that enable us to perceive the world as we've never seen before. We can now create psychosomatic health, shattering belief systems that once kept us bound to the illnesses, fates, and limitations of our ancestors.

We are the descendants of survivors, the cooperative ones, the firekeepers, and cave painters. But we are also the confused ones, the wanderers with smartphones glued to one hand and ancient fears gripped in the other. We are those dudes stumbling through late-stage capitalism with memes, trauma, and intermittent Wi-Fi, trying to remember who we are and why we're here. We are those dudes who point our fingers at others who are different, laugh at fart jokes, and theorize about quantum consciousness in the same breath. We meditate at dawn and doomscroll by night. We are paradox made visible, wisdom wrapped in denim, and spirit veiled in gilded sneakers.

But don't let the awkwardness fool you. These dudes—*we*—are not at the end of the line. We are the bridge. We are the hinge point. The goofy, glorious, in-progress prototypes of something luminous. Something tender and bold and unprecedented. Author Greg Braden sees us as forging pathways and writing the new human story.

Peace Prayer for Homo sapiens in Metamorphosis

Let us be at peace; while we ponder the notions, we are the wisdom carriers who sometimes forget to listen, and the miracle-makers who doubt their magic.
Let us be at peace while acknowledging that we are simultaneously the evolutionary inheritors of infinite, multidimensional, and universal expansion,
With both the volatile, emotional range of toddlers and the technological reach of the gods.

Let us be at peace, because today, while we know we are those dudes,
we also know we are preparing for much more.
We are preparing neurologically,
spiritually, and planetarily,
For a leap so profound, it will no doubt
render Homo sapiens a mere stepping stone to
Homo luminous and beyond.

CHAPTER FIVE
WE ARE THOSE BUTTERFLIES!

Turning our evolutionary kaleidoscope and peering through its sacred lens, we behold a dance of shifting panes, brilliant mosaics of color, and intricate, living geometry. Shapes shimmer, pulse, and reconfigure, revealing glimpses of the raw materials of human life: cells unfolding, DNA strands spiraling like cosmic calligraphy, microtubules flickering with light.

As we give the kaleidoscope another gentle turn, the pattern changes again—and suddenly, a flurry of luminous butterflies bursts forth. Their iridescent wings and chaotic, yet choreographed, movements appear to carry messages from a higher octave of life. In that moment, we remember the butterfly, our most cherished metaphor for transformation. And now, it reveals itself again—not just as a symbol of rebirth but as a mirror of our metamorphosis. These are not ordinary butterflies; they are us, *we are those butterflies*. Emerging from the cocoon of old identities, we are becoming the soulful, spiritual/human beings of a new, radiant humanity.

The metamorphosis of the butterfly has long symbolized the transformation of the soul. Manly P. Hall[viii] refers to the Mystery Schools of Ancient Greece and pre-Christian traditions—guardians of sacred philosophy and hidden wisdom. According to these teachings, only the initiated disciples were entrusted with the great secret: that the forces of Nature and the abstract laws of the Universe were personified into gods and goddesses, not to mislead but to make truth accessible through myth and metaphor.

In this light, the figure of *Psyche*—the radiant, stunningly beautiful maiden of Greek mythology with wings of opalescent light—becomes a profoundly evocative emblem for our discussion of the soul's journey as it parallels with Homo sapiens in metamorphosis toward Homo luminous. In Nature, transformation occurs without *thought*. But in the human experience, the vital forces of natural law require our conscious participation. We must choose to evolve. We must meet the chrysalis willingly.

We begin as larvae—unawakened, disconnected from spirit, living in the trance of separation. The pupa stage starts when we step onto the path of consciousness-raising, when the soul begins its Holy Work of remembrance. Through meditation, healing, ritual, study, prayer, and countless other sacred practices, we dissolve what no longer serves—and give form to what is yet to come. In time, the butterfly emerges: opalescent, luminous, and exquisitely individual. As with any initiation into philosophy, Mystery School, or spiritual discipline, the wings we grow reflect the depth of our devotion. Their size, shape, and splendor are shaped by the effort, intention, and soul-fire we bring to the journey.

We are that soul. We are *Psyche,* the mythical maiden with iridescent wings of splendor and beauty. We are that butterfly—emerging from the cocoon of what has been, rising into the skies of what is possible.

Evolutionary biologist and futurist Elisabet Sahtouris beautifully describes a hidden miracle within the caterpillar: "disc-like aggregates of stem cells that biologists call *imaginal cells*—hidden away inside the caterpillar all its life, remaining undeveloped until the crisis of overeating, fatigue, and breakdown allows them to develop, gradually replacing the caterpillar with a butterfly."[ix] Like tiny visionaries, these imaginal cells hold the blueprint for what is to come. They lie dormant until the old form collapses under its unsustainable weight. It is during the breakdown that the breakthrough begins.

Elizabet Sahtouris and Barbara Marx Hubbard draw upon the chrysalis as a profound metaphor in their teachings and documentaries on evolution. In Hubbard's online course, *Evolutionary Metamorphosis*, she expands the metaphor from the individual to the collective. The chrysalis, she proposes, is not only personal—it is planetary. Our societies, systems, and species are in a state of sacred disassembly. Just as the caterpillar must dissolve to fly, humanity must also surrender what no longer serves so that the emerging blueprint of *Homo luminous* may rise.

Turning our evolutionary kaleidoscope toward the future, we glimpse luminous spiritual and human beings—thriving, resilient, and radiant. They have survived and flourished because they allowed themselves to be sparked into action by the evolutionary impulse and propelled forward by the sacred momentum of consciousness itself. From this vantage point, we too are inspired—and we find ourselves nodding in resonance with Teilhard de Chardin, who reminds us: *"The whole future of the Earth… depends on the awakening of our faith in the future."*[11]

Through this visionary lens, we become inspired to have faith in the future. We witness these future humans guided by altruistic, democratically inclined Evolutionaries and futurists—those who rose to serve as stewards of transformation. They have banded together, not in uniformity, but in unity—to educate, uplift, and awaken one another. In their cooperative devotion to growth, we see echoes of cellular intelligence: as individual cells evolved by forming communities to increase their shared awareness, so have these spiritual humans united to expand their collective consciousness.

These evolved beings have cultivated telepathic communication, ecological harmony, and a deep symbiosis with the cosmos. They know how to access energy, light, and information from the *Noosphere*—the Unified Field of consciousness—and use it to heal themselves, one another, and the planet. They are not only responding to divine and evolutionary forces—they are co-creating with them. With compassion as their compass, they cooperate effortlessly with loved ones and strangers alike, embodying a new planetary ethic.

---

11 Pierre Teilhard de Chardin (Letters to Mme Georges-Marie Haardt) n.d.

In their presence, we recognize the seeds of our potential. These beings assemble an illumined, sustainable, and empowered species—living freely in a quantum reality that is alive with miracles. They are the future—but they are also the mirror, calling us forward to remembering who we are becoming.

Blinded by this glorious vision, we turn our evolutionary kaleidoscope once more and witness an incredible array of shifting panes—opalescent colors and fractal forms dancing in sacred motion. As we peer deeper into this future view, we are reminded of astronaut Frank White's[12] provocative speculation: that two thousand years from now, when humanity looks back on this era of the Great Shift, it will be clear that *many* species of the genus *Homo* were evolving side by side.

White suggests that our current dominant form may more accurately be called *Homo egoicus*, a reflection of our deep entrenchment in egoic consciousness. From there, he proposes transitional classifications—*Homo transitionalis, Homo holisticus, Homo luminous*—as humanity evolves toward higher coherence and integration. White goes further, envisioning the emergence of a *new genus entirely*, which he names *Psyche Materialis—soul made manifest in matter*. He believes these future beings will possess fully activated, Christ-like light bodies: conscious, radiant, divine, and capable of 'walking on water, healing the sick, and raising the dead.'

From our current vantage point, such classifications might feel speculative—even fantastical. But from the distant perspective of future history, they may be obvious. What we now call *Homo sapiens* may one day be understood as a single phase in a much broader spectrum of human expression. Whether future historians identify us as *Homo egoicus, Homo transitionalis, Homo universalis,* or *Homo angelicus* may ultimately be a moot point. What matters is that we are standing on the threshold of luminal awareness, moving from three-dimensional egoic beings toward five-dimensional (and beyond) luminous consciousness. We are learning to co-create—to draw matter from mind, form from frequency, substance from Source.

---

12 (White 1998)

We Are Those Butterflies!

From this present-day perspective, as our innate genius begins to awaken, a new name arises—one that feels inclusive, aspirational, and aligned with our highest potential: *Supraconscious Creators*. As author Bletzer[13] notes, the prefix *"supra"* implies "above and beyond" and, at times, "within and without." A *Supraconscious Creator* is *permanently connected* to that greater Field of Intelligence, above and beyond, within and without.

These beings of the future will routinely manifest light, healing, and miracles—not as rare anomalies, but as natural and spontaneous expressions of aligned awareness. By attuning to both the Morphogenic Field, which carries the energetic blueprints of form and function, and the Noosphere —the evolving field of collective human consciousness — they will intuit knowledge with ease. Their awareness will transcend subconscious limitations, enabling them to access insights that were previously unknown and yet to be discovered.

We are currently in the early stages of this process. We are only beginning to realize that our thoughts *create* our reality. Many of us vacillate or are still caught in the ego's resistance—fearful of letting go, clinging to illusion, trying to survive in outdated paradigms of separation. Yet the evolutionary trajectory is clear. We are on track to realize our potential as we learn thoroughly; *"we do not merely have thoughts—we are thought."* And it is through thought—elevated, focused, love-infused thought—that our transformation will unfold.

The Superconscious Mind of the Supraconscious Creator will be focused and disciplined, grounded in harmony and purpose. There will be no room for self-effacing or self-destructive thoughts. The creative higher mind, which is loving and aligned with the soul's essence, will reign, while the lower egoic mind, rooted in fear and separation, will gently dissolve. Dis-ease, mental, emotional, physical, and spiritual, will fade as we align with the healing frequencies of our divine nature. These future species, evolving within the genus of Supraconscious Creators, will deliberately choose affirming, life-generating thoughts.

---

13 Bletzer 1986, 601-2

To walk this path now is to accelerate our emergence. The Holy Work of consciousness-raising *is* the ignition point. It sheds light, provides the energy, and offers the tools for humanity to ascend into its Homo-luminous and gloriously Divine expression. Guiding that transition—birthing Supraconscious Creators into being—is not only the task but the sacred mission of evolution itself.

CHAPTER SIX
ARE WE THOSE STARSEEDS?

Starseeds are souls who originated in other star systems, dimensions, or realms of consciousness beyond Earth. They have incarnated here into human bodies through traditional birth, often repeatedly, to assist humanity during times of great transition, especially the planetary shift into higher-dimensional awareness. Starseeds carry within them the codes of advanced civilizations and soul memories of harmony, wisdom, and galactic connection. These codes often lie dormant until awakened by spiritual initiations, life challenges, or resonance with cosmic teachings. When activated, Starseeds remember who they truly are, emissaries of light, here to midwife a new Earth.

Many Starseeds report feelings of not fitting in, a longing for "home" in the stars, heightened sensitivity to energy, and a deep inner knowing that their purpose extends beyond the confines of conventional life. They may also experience accelerated spiritual awakening, multidimensional contact, and an innate pull toward healing, teaching, and service.

Along with Starseeds, the concept of Hybrids is gaining more mainstream acceptance. Hybrids are beings who carry genetic, energetic, or soul-level integration of multiple lineages, often combining human DNA with that of extraterrestrial, interdimensional, elemental, or celestial origins. Genetic interweaving is believed to have occurred either in utero, through galactic seeding, or energetic merging. In metaphysical teachings,

Hybrids are considered evolutionary bridges, born to usher humanity into higher states of awareness, unity, and multidimensional embodiment.

While the concept has ancient mythological roots—appearing in tales of demigods, angels, and shapeshifters—it has gained renewed interest in recent decades through channelings, regression therapy, and Starseed awakenings. Many Hybrids are said to carry within them encoded memories, advanced spiritual technologies, and innate wisdom from their non-Earth lineages, which often include beings from Sirius, Pleiades, Arcturus, Andromeda, or Orion.

Psychologically, Hybrids may experience themselves as "different" from others at an early age. They are known to be more empathic, psychic, and sensitive to energy and injustice. They often report a sense of mission, homesickness for the stars, and an intuitive knowing that they are here to assist with the planetary shift. While sometimes isolating, this identity becomes empowering when understood as part of a sacred design.

Starseeds and Hybrids often feel different, empathic, intuitive, and purpose-driven. A Starseed may also be a Hybrid if their soul chose a biologically integrated incarnation that includes star-being genetics. Both carry encoded wisdom and frequencies designed to activate higher consciousness within themselves and in others.

When viewed through our kaleidoscope for becoming and through the lens of CP, Starseeds, and Hybrids are not anomalies; they are prototypes. They represent the merging of human and cosmic intelligence, the convergence of the physical and the supra-physical or supernatural. They are understood not as escapists from another galaxy but as sacred seed-bearers of evolution. They signal that evolution is no longer just biological; it is energetic, soulful, and galactic in scope. Their presence helps anchor higher frequencies into the Earth's collective field, known as the Noosphere. As more awaken to their origin and mission, the planetary kaleidoscope turns again, illuminating humanity's connection to the greater galactic family. These identities are expressions of soul-level specialization, representing archetypal roles within the grand evolutionary symphony. Whether Starseed, Hybrid, or both, they are here to help humanity remember its own cosmic origin and luminous potential.

A Note about Walk-ins, Reptilians, Tricksters, Greys, and Elementals

A *Walk-In* refers to the phenomenon where one soul leaves a physical body and another soul, usually of a more evolved, angelic, or ultra-terrestrial nature, enters to continue the incarnation. This concept dates to ancient Hindu literature, which was understood as a kind of soul merging or substitution, often to fulfill a divine mission or accelerate planetary evolution. Walk-ins may occur following near-death experiences, spiritual crises, or profound initiatory moments. On a soul level, the incoming soul typically agrees to take over the "contract" of the departing soul, often bringing advanced wisdom, healing capacities, or cosmic perspective.

The need for discernment has never been greater as we expand our individual and collective consciousness. Energetic sovereignty and spiritual clarity are vital. Actual walk-in experiences often bring not only an expanded awareness but also a deepened commitment to service, coherence, and love. They are not escapes from life but sacred realignments with a higher purpose.

However, not all walk-in experiences are beneficial or benign. Some walk-ins may be trickster energies or lesser-evolved entities masquerading as beings of light, seeking to access the physical realm for their own agendas. These can include certain extraterrestrial or ultra-dimensional beings who mimic higher frequencies but do not serve the soul's evolution.

Tricksters are ancient, archetypal figures found in mythologies worldwide. They appear as animals, humans, spirits, or gods who disrupt order, bend the rules, and reveal hidden truths through chaos, mischief, or inversion. In traditional stories, they are agents of transformation, challenging norms and catalyzing unexpected growth. Coyote in Native American lore, Loki in Norse mythology, and Anansi in West African stories are classic examples.

In contemporary spiritual discourse, particularly within the New Age and metaphysical communities, the term "trickster" has acquired a more cautionary connotation. It is increasingly used to describe supernatural or interdimensional entities that pose as light beings or ascended guides but carry deceptive or self-serving intentions. These entities may lure seekers through flattery, false promises, or energetic mimicry, encouraging channeling, dependency, or, in extreme cases, energetic possession.

When viewed through our evolutionary kaleidoscope for becoming and through the lens of CP, tricksters are seen as part of the broader ecosystem of consciousness. They do not necessarily represent "evil" but rather unintegrated shadows within the psyche and the cosmos. Their presence calls for discernment, boundary-setting, and inner alignment. They may appear when the ego seeks shortcuts, trauma seeks relief, or the seeker is ready to encounter and transcend illusion.

True spiritual empowerment comes not from fearing the trickster but from recognizing the vibration of truth. When the heart is coherent and the light body activated, tricksters lose their power to deceive.

Recognizing the vibration of truth with discernment is also paramount for dealing with Reptilians. Also referred to as reptilian humanoids, reptiloids, octopoids, archons, or draconians, Reptilians are a purported race of extraterrestrial or interdimensional beings said to either covertly inhabit Earth or influence it through psychic or physical possession of human hosts, particularly those in positions of political or corporate power. Within certain conspiracy-based metaphysical narratives, they are believed to have an agenda of control, domination, or energetic harvesting. Their sudden appearance in a human host may coincide with behavioral changes, dissociation, or symptoms that resemble psychiatric disturbances, especially psychosis and dissociative identity disorder.

Some psychics and energy healers report seeing these beings in subtle or shadow forms within individuals' auras or energetic fields, often during healing sessions or psychic scans.

Dr. Meg Blackburn Losey details her experiences removing these entities in her book *Touching the Light*. She suggests visualizing a lightsaber and emphasizes that once the entity is removed, the key to permanent healing for the entity and the host is to hold the entity up to the light and send it home.

Dr. Phil Mollon has written an extensive and scholarly book on removing energetic parasites and helping clients release attachments, titled *Blue Diamond Healing*. Dr. Mollon has devoted his career to energy psychology and was the first president of the Association for Comprehensive Energy Psychology (ACEP). On page 117, he writes, "Most healthy people do not have energy parasites... identifying the particular variety of parasite is not essential." Transmuting the sabotaging, misery-producing energy with love is always the primary approach.

When viewed through a symbolic or psychological lens, particularly within the frameworks of Energy Psychology and Celestial Psychology, the Reptilian archetype can be interpreted as a metaphor for undeveloped or un-integrated consciousness. It reflects the domination of the reptilian brain, the oldest part of the human nervous system, which governs fear, aggression, and survival instincts. In this view, "Reptilians" represent individuals or aspects of ourselves that resist evolution, cling to control, and operate solely from lower-frequency motivations.

Whether understood as literal beings, energetic parasites, or archetypes of the unawakened ego, the concept of Reptilians invites a deeper inquiry into power, sovereignty, and the spiritual imperative to evolve beyond fear-based consciousness.

The *Greys*, also known as Zeta Reticulans or Grey aliens, are among the most frequently reported extraterrestrial beings in UFO and contactee lore. They are typically described as small-bodied, thin, with large heads, grayish skin, and oversized black eyes devoid of visible pupils. In mainstream ufology, Greys are said to originate from the Zeta Reticuli star system and are frequently associated with abduction narratives, genetic experiments, and telepathic communication. Accounts range from cold, clinical interactions to more benevolent encounters designed to support humanity.

Within metaphysical and spiritual frameworks, the nature of the Greys is a subject of debate. Some believe they are technologically advanced but emotionally underdeveloped beings who seek to reconnect with their spiritual essence by working with human DNA. Others consider them to be bioengineered emissaries, neutral observers, or even trickster entities operating outside human moral frameworks.

Through the lens of the kaleidoscope of becoming, or the perspectives of CP, the Greys represent the risks of technological advancement without emotional or spiritual integration. Whether literal beings or archetypal messengers, they invite us to contemplate what it means to evolve as heart-centered, intelligent, and multidimensional beings. They symbolize the cautionary tale of technological advancement without heart-centered evolution.

Elemental Beings are spirits or consciousness forms associated with the primal forces of nature, earth, air, fire, and water. Elemental Beings are found in many mythological and esoteric traditions. Often depicted as gnomes (earth), sylphs (air), salamanders (fire), and undines (water), they are said to inhabit the subtle realms, working in harmony with Gaia's living body to maintain the balance of ecosystems and natural cycles. In a broader metaphysical sense, they are understood as vibrational intelligences that embody the sacred choreography of the natural world. While rarely perceived with the physical senses, they may be intuited during deep meditative states or through spontaneous experiences of wonder, reverence, or communion with the natural world. Honoring these beings affirms the soul's alliance with Earth's aliveness.

In the ever-shifting kaleidoscope of multidimensional consciousness, humanity is not alone in its evolutionary unfolding. Throughout history, and especially in this age of awakening, reports of contact with non-human intelligence have surged into public awareness. From benevolent walk-ins, who arrive through soul-level agreements to assist with planetary transformation, to the shadowy presence of Reptilians and Greys, often associated with control-based paradigms, these beings invite us to expand our perceptions of reality and deepen our spiritual discernment. In contrast, Elemental Beings—nature spirits and vibrational stewards of the Earth—remind us of our innate kinship with the living world. Within the lens of CP, these entities are not reduced to binary judgments of good or evil but are explored as archetypal forces, vibrational presences, and evolutionary catalysts. Their appearance mirrors our inner awakening processes, whether experienced literally, symbolically, or in visionary states. This chapter is less about "believing in aliens" and more about recognizing the holographic complexity of consciousness and our courageous role in evolving with it.

CHAPTER SEVEN
WE ARE THE EVOLUTION OF OUR BECOMING!

*Evolution is a consciousness-raising experience.*ˣ
—Hubbard

We are beginning to realize something both ancient and brand-new: *evolution is not just happening to us—we are participating in it.* Thanks to breakthroughs in science, psychology, technology, philosophy, and alternative energy medicine, we now understand that evolution *is* consciousness in motion. And even more radically, we are becoming conscious of our role in the evolutionary process.

As Barbara Marx Hubbard envisioned, "We ourselves are beginning to consciously become quantum field co-creators, using our thoughts to energize and direct everything from the snowflake to distant quasars—to phase them into harmony with the Father Universe." We are not passive passengers on a biological ride—we are conscious Creators, awakening to our power to shape reality itself. From supercharged brains and luminous bodies to the evolutionary arc of our species, we are learning that we can influence it all—deliberately, intentionally, and energetically.

If you ask cellular biologist and epigenetics pioneer Bruce Lipton, he'll tell you the human brain is already preparing for a quantum leap.

"We're establishing new neural pathways, exploring neuro-architectures that allow us to perceive in ways we've never perceived before. This is what allows us to create psychosomatic health—not just psychosomatic disease—to shatter the belief structures that have crippled us for generations, keeping us trapped in the genetic patterns of our ancestors."

In other words, the leap is not only planetary—it is neurological. Evolution is no longer just a matter of biological adaptation. It is now a conscious, psycho-spiritual activation. We are the bridge between the past and the future of infinite possibilities. *We are the evolution of our own becoming.*

Peering once again into the tube of our evolutionary kaleidoscope, we discover something wondrous: a new breed of *Homo sapiens* is already among us. They are known as Evolutionaries, a classification that can include Lightworkers, Earthkeepers, Starseeds, metaphysicians, holistic & energy medicine practitioners—the imaginal cells of the chrysalis, quietly shaping the future from within.

These Evolutionaries are not just observing change; they participate in it, consciously co-creating the next phase of human development. Starseeds and Lightworkers, in particular, recognize and, therefore, realize emerging aspects of the Human Energy System (HES) that were once hidden, dormant, or dismissed as myth. Among these are the God's Mouth Chakra, the Star Chakras, and the multidimensional toroidal fields associated with the Merkabah. The increasing visibility and vocabulary around these energy structures do more than chart the evolution of the light body—they signify the evolution of our creative capacities.

The process of naming something is to call it into being. And when we focus our awareness on these subtle structures—when we speak of them, write about them, teach them, and channel them —they begin to shimmer into greater coherence and accessibility. This is how evolution works at the quantum level:

Consciousness-focused equals reality forged.

The God's Mouth Chakra is a primary example. It is seated just behind the soft palate and has emerged as a vital portal of divine expression, a gateway for higher-order communication, healing resonance, and encoded speech. As we awaken to these new energetic architectures, we also awaken to new creative authority—one that invites us to speak from the soul, not just the throat. For an in-depth exploration of the God's Mouth Chakra and its role in the new human anatomy, see Appendix One.

Evolutionaries are individuals who view all of creation through evolutionary eyes. They see the Universe as a living, sacred process, not a static design. For them, evolution is not merely a biological function but a spiritual unfolding—far more inclusive than the limitations of classical Darwinian theory. They understand that the transformation of our world depends on our willingness to *consciously* and *deliberately* evolve. Our species and planet's survival hinges on this sacred process.

By nature, Evolutionaries are committed to this path of becoming. They know that evolution is not separate from them, but rather a living process through which they exist. They recognize that consciousness expands its capacity to know itself and experience reality *through us*. Whether we identify as Evolutionaries or not, the process is underway for all of us. Those drawn to books such as this one, as well as philosophy, psychology, or sociology studies, are likely part of this emerging lineage.

And those of us who engage in psychology—the art of making the unconscious conscious, the study of the soul—are by nature *conscious Evolutionaries*. Our growing curiosity about the self, the psyche, and the mechanics of awareness is helping us, as Barbara Marx Hubbard beautifully said, to "lace the broad perspective"—to weave together the great evolutionary story with the personal human journey.

To develop evolutionary eyes is to awaken to a broader view: to see that we are not just living through change—we are participating in evolution's design. This shift in awareness is nothing short of revolutionary.

Kaleidoscope for Becoming: A Grimoire of Revolution

As philosopher Carter Phipps reminds us:

"Our emerging understanding of evolution is so transformative that eventually, every important area of human life will fall under its revelatory spell. It will change the way we think about life, culture, consciousness—even thinking itself—for the better. In fact, it already is."

Turning the kaleidoscope again, we discover the transformative vision that Carter Phipps calls the evolutionary worldview. With new evolutionary eyes, we begin to perceive meaning and purpose embedded in every layer of life. Whether our lens focuses on the microcosm of our individual journeys or the macrocosm of our collective unfolding, everything we observe reflects the process of conscious improvement. We recognize that our true mission is to further the evolution of the world we chose to be born into.

The evolutionary worldview allows us to participate fully in the world without being attached. We take up our causes without taking them personally, making us more effective, compassionate, and sovereign as change-makers. We learn to see beyond the surface of negativity and instead recognize the silver lining in every cloud. Adopting a melioristic perspective, we understand that what comes to the surface in pain or chaos is doing so for purification and transformation. Disasters, whether natural or man-made—social, political, economic, emotional, or physical—all begin to *make sense* within the forward movement of evolutionary design. We no longer see the struggle as punishment but as a necessary birth canal for new consciousness.

This sacred idea is not new. The occultists and mystics of the ancient world had a remarkable understanding of evolution, not just as a physical process but as a universal principle of becoming. They believed that all of life existed in various stages of spiritual evolution: grains of sand in the process of becoming human (in consciousness, if not in form), humans becoming planets, planets becoming cosmic chains, and onward—*ad infinitum*.

We are the Evolution of our Becoming!

Crucially, the evolutionary worldview acknowledges that even our most profound spiritual intuitions are not static. They are not fixed truths handed down for all time; they evolve as history progresses. Consciousness is not simply waking up—it is unfolding, deepening, spiraling upward.

Although this principle has existed since antiquity, it was only in the past century that it was named and embraced as the evolutionary worldview. This worldview, as Phipps writes, *"will constitute the organizing principle of a new worldview, uniquely suited for the twenty-first century and beyond."* It reflects a growing synthesis—an Age of Interspirituality—where an exponential convergence of scientific, psychological, and spiritual insight emerges.

FORGING THE LUMINOUS BLUEPRINT

Over the past twenty years, signal-transduction biologists have studied the intelligence and behavior of the cell's Integral Membrane Proteins (IMPs). Lipton proposed that the membrane, not the nucleus, is the actual brain of the cell, housing these IMPs, which exhibit intelligent decision-making behaviors. The two fundamental types of IMPs are the receptor proteins (which receive information) and the effector proteins (which act on that information). Lipton refers to these units as cellular "perception," which creates "physical sensation,"[xi] known as *manifestation* in metaphysical circles.

This behavior of microscopic IMPs invites a macro view that mirrors human behavior. Raising consciousness involves improving both our receptor and effector capacities. The more aware we become of our beliefs, stories, and patterns, the better equipped we are to choose new actions that align with our higher intelligence. Just as cells become "smarter" by refining and expanding the surface area of their membranes to allow for more receptor-effector interactions, so do we evolve through meditation and visualization techniques designed to develop our Luminous Energy Field (LEF) and our Human Energy System (HES).

Through these practices, we increase our capacity to perceive and respond wisely. We stretch our auric bodies toward greater intelligence. We become wiser and more luminous by design, consciously expanding our energetic membranes, just as the earliest cells once did in response to evolutionary pressure. This, too, is natural selection on the level of the soul. As we turn the lens of our transcendent, visionary, evolutionary kaleidoscope once more, a stunning future vision comes into view—a revelation shimmering at the edge of possibility. We behold a time when the luminous-energetic body of the spiritual/human being is not merely stirred into wakefulness but is fully activated, coherent, congruent, and sovereign. We are discovering this is not some distant fantasy but a he glimpse of tnext octave of human evolution.

We are the Evolution of our Becoming!

In this radiant future, the aura is no longer a faint shimmer seen by mystics; it is a vibrant, multidimensional field of light and intelligence, pulsing with color, pattern, and purpose. All auric layers of the auric field, from the emotional to the causal, from the etheric to the astral, are awake and interactive, functioning as a dynamic interface between the soul and the body. These layers are radiant living *mem-brains* of memory and intelligence. They are not merely protective sheaths; they are sophisticated, responsive systems that encode the wisdom of lifetimes and transmit the frequencies of higher consciousness through each consecutive layer, ultimately reaching the physical body on a cellular level. This vision is not just an upgrade of human biology but a luminous prophecy of what becomes possible when we learn to live as frequency-aware, soul-integrated beings.

In this model, the *Integral Membrane Proteins* of our etheric body are mirrored in the intelligence-gathering activities of our chakras. Like a receptor-effector unit, each energy center processes and transmits divine data. Take chakra six, for example—its receptor activity connects with the pineal gland, located in the prefrontal cortex, forming a higher circuitry of perception that bridges the biological and the mystical. The beings of our evolutionary future have auras that are clear of psychic debris, vibrant with rainbow hues, and visible to the naked eye. Their chakras are balanced, spinning in perfect harmony, and their psychic faculties are fully awakened.

Around each of them spins a luminous toroidal field, a vortex of living energy. They are wrapped in a Merkabah-like vehicle of golden light, designed for healing, Ascension, and multidimensional travel. These Homo-luminous beings are not fantasy. They are an emerging reality already seeded within our DNA, whispering through our dreams, visions, and meditations. In them, we see a humanity capable of healing itself and others, manifesting abundance, and living cooperatively, joyously, and peacefully. They operate at higher frequencies, specifically gamma brainwaves, as a permanent state. They govern themselves not by laws or fear but by the frequencies of higher consciousness. Their luminous mem-brains govern the health of their cells, just as their awakened consciousness links them to the mem-brain of the Universal Body—the *Noosphere*.

These images, shown to us by another gentle turn of our future-facing magic kaleidoscope, reveal this exquisite new evolutionary scene. While it may seem like science fiction, it is becoming increasingly relevant to contemporary science. *It is the dawn of Homo luminous.*

And just as we once rose from four legs to two and learned to outwit the saber-toothed tiger, we are now rising in consciousness to face down a new set of threats—chemical pollutants, nuclear hazards, emotional overload, and the heavy imprint of collective trauma. Once upon a time, evolution was about muscle and adaptation. Today, it demands something far more refined—intelligence, innovation, the 12 Codes of the Evolutionary Trajectory, and conscious co-creation of our Luminous Energy Fields (LEF) and our Human Energy Systems (HES).

Through our work in consciousness-raising and the concepts in CP, we understand that Quality of Life (QOL) is directly proportional to the quantity of Light, Energy, and Information (QOLEI) that we consciously receive, integrate, and emit.

$\wedge$ QOL α $\wedge$ QOLEI x QQ-CEFV

This sacred equation is not just philosophical; it is experiential. When we engage in healing practices like *13th Octave LaHoChi* with presence, devotion, and coherence, we participate in a vibrational loop of Reciprocal Nourishment. Our joy, gratitude, and willingness become energetic offerings that feed the very Beings assisting us, amplifying their capacity to support us in return. This sacred equation becomes embodied when we engage with presence and coherence, creating a vibrational loop of Reciprocal Nourishment—an energy exchange in which we are both the receivers and the radiators of evolutionary support. In this way, Reciprocal Nourishment becomes a lived expression of the QOL formula, demonstrating that the more attuned we are to the currents of light and energy, the more luminous, meaningful, and supported our lives become.

In this co-creative field, healing is no longer a plea or petition. It becomes a radiant conversation with the Divine, a communion across dimensions. The beings who assist us, be they guides, Ascended Masters, or nonhuman intelligence, are also nourished by our joy, gratitude, and willingness to evolve. In rare and profound moments, this communion may open what experiencer Chris Bledsoe and others have called a "temporal connection," a telepathic bridge across space, time, and dimension, enabling direct communication with higher intelligence. Bledsoe is a contactee whose encounters are so deeply resonant and vibrationally coherent that he has drawn the attention of scientists, spiritual leaders, and intelligence agencies alike. He is hailed as a *living conduit*—a human whose luminous field serves as a threshold between worlds.

These are not mere fantasies of contact, but sacred entrainments of consciousness. They indicate a soul-level resonance echoing between now and elsewhere, here and beyond.

Such connections are made possible by the very light body we are cultivating, our inner technology of multidimensional awareness. Temporal connections, then, are not external phenomena but inner permissions. They arise when the frequency is ripe, our chakra system is coherent, and our luminous body vibrates in harmonic sympathy with other realms. Temporal connection is not a matter of fantasy or imagination; it is a frequency-based reality. It is not bound by time but by tone, by the harmonic resonance between consciousnesses attuned to the same sacred frequency. When the soul vibrates in harmony with the unseen and radiates coherence, timelines dissolve, and communion with the unseen, including the Divine, begins.

Kaleidoscope for Becoming: A Grimoire of Revolution

The following pages contain affirmations designed to enhance the vitality and coherence of each chakra, supporting your evolutionary upgrade—not just for healing, but also for contact, clarity, communication, coherence, and communion.

We are the Evolution of our Becoming!

Chakra One ~~ Affirmations to Enhance Our Becoming

For Chakra One, think of the color red, the element earth, the seed sound Lam, and the musical note "C."

Call upon the Great Cosmic Reweaver, Hunab Ku, and visualize this glorious Mayan Galactic Butterfly enhancing your metamorphosis.

Repeat these Affirmations three times a day for thirty days.

I am safe because the first chakra of my energetic/spiritual body is activated, open, and alive.

I am a spiritual being having a human experience.

I chose to have this human experience.

I know this is true because deep down, I know myself as infinite, cooperative, empathic,

compassionate, and illumined.

I have purpose and value.

I am capable of healing myself and others.

My first chakra is balanced and

spinning in its perfect direction

for where I am right now, working toward my evolution,

and strengthening my

Human Energy System, creating my Luminous Energy Field,

activating my Homo-luminous being.

Notes:

_____
_____
_____

We are the Evolution of our Becoming!

Chakra Two ~~ Affirmations to Enhance Our Becoming

Chakras ~ Energy System
Transformation Stations

Chakra Two

Svadhisthana
One's Own Place

For Chakra Two, think of the color orange, the element water, the seed sound Vam, and the musical note "D."

Call upon the Great Cosmic Reweaver, Hunab Ku, and visualize this glorious Mayan Galactic Butterfly enhancing your metamorphosis.

Repeat these Affirmations three times a day for thirty days.

I am successful because the second chakra of my energetic/spiritual body is activated, open, and alive.

I change myself by raising my awareness to a higher consciousness.

I have the freedom to transform my humanness into a Divine Self or Higher Self.

I use the power of my second chakra to achieve the success I need to change.

My second chakra allows me to achieve mastery over my humanness in all ways.

My emotions and my creativity blossom and flow. All my senses are activated.

My second chakra is balanced and spinning in its perfect direction for where I am right now, working toward my evolution, and strengthening my

Human Energy System, creating my Luminous Energy Field, activating my Homo-luminous being.

Notes:
_____
_____
_____

We are the Evolution of our Becoming!

Chakra Three ~~ Affirmations to Enhance Our Becoming

For Chakra Three, think of the color yellow, the element fire, the seed sound Ram, and the musical note "E."

Call upon the Great Cosmic Reweaver, Hunab Ku, and visualize this glorious Mayan Galactic Butterfly enhancing your metamorphosis.

Repeat these Affirmations three times a day for thirty days.

I am powerful because the third chakra of my energetic/spiritual body is activated, open, and alive. I am driven to evolve.

I work with the power of my third chakra to awaken my transformation to a Homo-luminous being.

All my actions are governed by my right to act in ways that produce the energy, vitality, and personal power necessary to complete this transformation.

I choose only that which is good for me, and my boundaries keep me confident and strong in self-value.

My third chakra is balanced and
spinning in its perfect direction
for where I am right now, working toward my evolution,
and strengthening my
Human Energy System, creating my Luminous Energy Field,
activating my Homo-luminous being.

Notes:
_____
_____
_____

We are the Evolution of our Becoming!

Chakra Four ~~ Affirmations to Enhance Our Becoming

For Chakra Four, think of the color green, the element air, the seed sound Yam, and the musical note "F."

Call upon the Great Cosmic Reweaver, Hunab Ku, and visualize this glorious Mayan Galactic Butterfly enhancing your metamorphosis.

Repeat these Affirmations three times a day for thirty days.

I am loving because the fourth chakra of my energetic/spiritual body is activated, open, and alive.

I am appropriately open and loving toward everyone and everything.

I extend forgiveness to the best of my ability,
as I work toward my complete and ultimate healing.

I am connected to the Universe.

I am connected to the Divine.

My fourth chakra makes this connection easily and freely by giving and receiving love.

My fourth chakra is balanced and spinning in its perfect direction for where I am right now, working toward my evolution, and strengthening my
Human Energy System, creating my Luminous Energy Field, activating my Homo-luminous being.

Notes:

_____
_____
_____

We are the Evolution of our Becoming!

Chakra Five ~~ Affirmations to enhance our becoming:

For Chakra Five, think of the color blue, the element ether, the seed sound Ham, and the musical note "G."

Call upon the Great Cosmic Reweaver, Hunab Ku, and visualize this glorious Mayan Galactic Butterfly enhancing your metamorphosis.

Repeat these Affirmations three times a day for thirty days.

I am communicative because the fifth chakra of my energetic/spiritual body is activated, open, and alive.

I love to practice the Holy Work of
consciousness-raising for myself and others.

I communicate clearly, logically,
and truthfully about all areas of my life.

I am assertive and effective.

I speak truths that raise the consciousness of others,
as well as my own.

I use my voice to assist in the evolution of humankind.
I listen closely, carefully, and deeply.

My fifth chakra is balanced and spinning in its perfect
direction for where I am right now, working toward my
evolution, and strengthening my
Human Energy System, creating my Luminous Energy Field,
activating my Homo-luminous being.

Notes:
_____
_____
_____

We are the Evolution of our Becoming!

Chakra Six ~~ Affirmations to enhance our becoming:

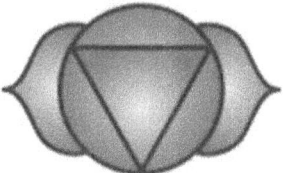

For Chakra Six, think of the color indigo, the element ether, the seed sound Om, and the musical note "A."

Call upon the Great Cosmic Reweaver, Hunab Ku, and visualize this glorious Mayan Galactic Butterfly enhancing your metamorphosis.

Repeat these Affirmations three times a day for thirty days.

I am creative because the sixth chakra of my energetic/spiritual body is activated, open, and alive.
I co-create with the Divine.
I co-create my reality.

**The more Holy Work I do, the more I know the Divine.
I create a miraculous life.**

I create miracles for myself and others.

I can see with my mind's eye all that is Divine.

My mind is sharp, powerful, creative, and brilliant.

I know all things because my mind is one with the Divine.

**My sixth chakra is balanced and spinning in its perfect direction for where I am right now, working toward my evolution, and strengthening my
Human Energy System, creating my Luminous Energy Field, activating my Homo-luminous being.**

Notes:
_____
_____
_____

We are the Evolution of our Becoming!

Chakra Seven ~~ Affirmations to enhance our becoming:

Chakras – Energy System
Transformation Stations

Chakra Seven

Sahasrara
"Thousandfold"

For Chakra Seven, think of the color purple, the element consciousness, the seed sound Ng, and the musical note "B."

Call upon the Great Cosmic Reweaver, Hunab Ku, and visualize this glorious Mayan Galactic Butterfly enhancing your metamorphosis.

Repeat these Affirmations three times a day for thirty days.

I am transcendent because the seventh chakra of my energetic/spiritual body is activated, open, and alive. I am transcendent and one with the infinite.

I am free from the trappings of the egoic mind.

I am timeless and eternal.

I am the source of everything.

I have no beginning, and I have no end.

I am all that ever was, and I am all that ever will be.

I am the infinite potentiality, the inexhaustible possibility.

My flow is eternal, all-reaching, unhindered by time or space.

My seventh chakra is balanced and spinning in its perfect direction for where I am right now, working toward my evolution, and strengthening my Human Energy System, creating my Luminous Energy Field, activating my Homo-luminous being.

Notes:

Chakra Eight ~~ Affirmations to enhance our becoming:

For Chakra Eight, think of the color iridescent lavender, the element fire, the seed sound Hrim (pronounced Hreem), and the musical note "G#."

Call upon the Great Cosmic Reweaver, Hunab Ku, and visualize this glorious Mayan Galactic Butterfly enhancing your metamorphosis.

Repeat these Affirmations three times a day for thirty days.

I am zealous about spirituality because the eighth chakra of my energetic and spiritual body is activated, open, and alive.

I expand and merge with the Divine.

I channel higher consciousness with ease.

I am intuitive and temporally connected
to multidimensional and extraterrestrial existence.

I access Akashic records and cleanse and
clear karma with ease.

I am a lucid dreamer.

I express my divine wisdom harmoniously and effortlessly.

My eighth chakra is balanced and spinning in its perfect direction for where I am right now, working toward my evolution, and strengthening my
Human Energy System, creating my Luminous Energy Field, activating my Homo-luminous being.

Notes:
_____
_____
_____

CHAPTER EIGHT
EVEN SCIENCE, PSYCHOLOGY, AND SPIRITUALITY ARE BECOMING!

The disciplines of science, psychology, and spirituality are fusing into a unified field of consciousness, and Holomovement is a model that provides evidence of this without doubt. Physicist David Bohm's concept of intricate order laid the groundwork for understanding the interconnected, dynamic reality beneath all appearances. Science is now catching up to what mystics have long known. Everything is connected, and every aspect of nature and the universe contains a fractal of the whole, mirroring the intelligence of consciousness itself. Quantum entanglement and non-locality demonstrate that science is evolving into a more spiritual realm, embracing a broader worldview that encompasses intention, the observer effect, and coherent resonance.

One of the most recent and influential books on Holomovement is *The Holomovement: Embracing Our Collective Purpose to Unite Humanity*, published in 2023. This anthology, edited by Emanuel Kuntzelman and Jill Robinson, features contributions from thought leaders such as Jude Currivan, Duane Elgin, Ervin Laszlo, Lynne Twist, and Ken Wilber. The book explores the Holomovement as a unifying worldview that integrates scientific, spiritual, aesthetic, and artistic perspectives, emphasizing our interconnectedness and collective evolution.

The Holomovement can be seen as the shift from reductionist models of the mind to integrative, holistic frameworks, such as transpersonal psychology, somatic therapies, Energy Psychology, and *Celestial Psychology*®. As the psyche is increasingly understood as multidimensional and vibrational, we are witnessing psychology evolve into *a spiritual science* capable of mapping pathology and the radiant architecture of the soul.

The growing interest in the Holomovement as a framework for understanding and fostering unity across all domains and among all disciplines further indicates humanity's evolutionary uptick in consciousness. It is more than a metaphor; it presents a new story, showing us that reality is not made up of separate parts, but of dynamic wholeness in motion. It teaches us that a field of deep interconnectedness lies beneath every boundary—a living flow where matter, mind, and meaning co-arise. As this realization seeps into the collective psyche, it ripples through every domain: physics, medicine, education, ecology. But perhaps nowhere is it more poetically expressed than in the realm of spirit. If the universe itself is a unified field of consciousness in motion, then every spiritual path is a tributary of the same great river. This concept is the essence of Interspirituality, which is not a melting pot of traditions but a holographic flowering, where each practice, prayer, and lineage carries a glimmer of the Whole. Just as every particle contains the cosmos, so too does every sacred tradition contain a seed of universal truth.

As we continue to turn our paradigm-shifting evolutionary kaleidoscope, we glimpse new patterns emerging in spirituality: an all-encompassing, all-inclusive, and forward-moving spirituality. Kurt Johnson and David Robert Ord refer to this movement as Interspirituality, describing it as *"the movement of all discussions—especially those related to who we are, why we are here, and where we are going—toward the experience of profound interconnectedness, unity consciousness, and oneness."*

Interspirituality is the natural discussion among human beings about what we are experiencing. In academic terms, it's the intersubjective discussion among us all about who we are, why we are here, and where we are going. In the context of religion, Interspirituality is the common heritage of humankind's spiritual wisdom and the sharing of wisdom resources across traditions. In terms of our developing human consciousness, Interspirituality is the movement of all these discussions toward the experience of profound interconnectedness, unity consciousness, and oneness.[xii]

This ascending spirituality is patterned as a spiral, one of the oldest symbols of sacred growth. We see it in the unfolding of consciousness itself and reflected in the progression of psychological theory and human potential.

From Freud to Maslow to today's integrative thinkers, modern psychology has consistently built upon itself, always in service of improving human experience, making life 'better and better, every day in every way.' Making conscious what is unconscious remains the cornerstone of all self-transformation, whether driven by psychotherapy or spirituality. Consciousness-raising first took root in the Western psyche when Freud invited his patients to speak freely—to bring the shadow sludge of their inner world into the light. Maslow's self-actualization principles continue to underpin all our efforts toward meaning-making and personal growth.

Today, transpersonal psychology, metaphysics, and New Thought are no longer fringe pursuits, and they are converging with evolutionary frameworks to form an emergent discipline of *conscious evolution*. The integrative field recognizes that human transformation is not a side effect of evolution; it is its very purpose. As envisioned by pioneers such as Sri Aurobindo and Pierre Teilhard de Chardin, the aim of evolution is not merely survival or adaptation, but the flowering of a human being who, through self-awareness, self-determination, and self-regulation, fully embodies and radiates the inner life of the Spirit.

In this light, consciousness, psychology, spirituality, and evolution are not isolated domains but interwoven strands of a single sacred braid. Each contributes to the awakening of a species capable of co-creating its own future—not through domination, but through divine participation.

Gregg Braden asserts that traditional teachings of Darwinian evolution are no longer sufficient to explain the profound inner transformations occurring within us. He reminds us, "Almost universally, scriptures from the world's most ancient and cherished spiritual traditions agree that we humans are linked to something beyond ourselves and our immediate surroundings" (p. 100). These ancestral echoes affirm what science is only beginning to grasp: that we are more than biology; we are bridges between worlds.

East and West, once perceived as opposite poles, are now entering into a creative fusion. The contemplative wisdom of the East—its stillness, its surrender—is meeting the dynamic drive of the West—its innovation, its will to become. From this union, a new facet of spirituality is birthing. It is not a religion but a rhythm. A spirituality that evolves as we evolve, including everyone and every ideology without diluting and uplifting without bypassing. It is the soul of evolution awakening to itself. It is the Universe getting to know itself through us.

Even Science, Psychology, and Spirituality are Becoming!

EVOLUTIONARY ENLIGHTENMENT

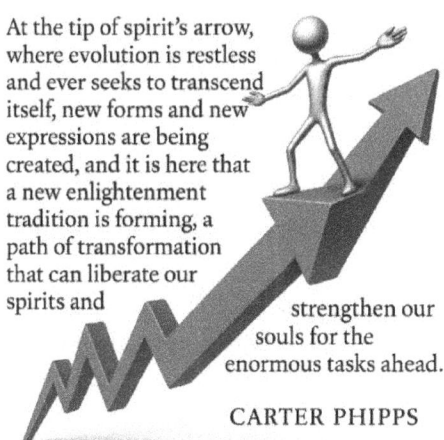

At the tip of spirit's arrow, where evolution is restless and ever seeks to transcend itself, new forms and new expressions are being created, and it is here that a new enlightenment tradition is forming, a path of transformation that can liberate our spirits and strengthen our souls for the enormous tasks ahead.

CARTER PHIPPS

Thanks to the natural trajectory of evolution toward improvement and philosophers like Ken Wilber, Andrew Cohen, and Carter Phipps, enlightenment is becoming recognized as an achievable goal for everyone.

"Enlightenment, this elusive state, has been the focus of some of the greatest minds throughout history. Thousands of people have dedicated their lives to its pursuit. We believe that enlightenment promises everyone the possibility for innovation, extraordinary creativity, and inner peace."[xiii]

The most literal definition of enlightenment is "to illumine." The Enlightenment Era, also known as the European Age of Enlightenment, originated in the mid-1600s. Philosophers of that time were not enlightened beings in the way we think of Christ, Buddha, or the Dalai Lama; however, their lives and demonstrated works created a significant elevation in consciousness, paving the way for our current New Age Shift. Kant chose emergence (as in metamorphosis) in his saying, "Enlightenment is man's emergence from his self-incurred immaturity." Self-incurred immaturity reminds us of Hall's "unregenerate man, ignorant and helpless" in the caterpillar larva stage. These philosophers sought to educate the masses and overturn the dogmatic, illogical, and intolerant ideologies primarily generated by religious doctrine, which dominated European thinking. Replacing outdated ideals with scientific, democratic, and altruistic ones parallels today's emerging Interspiritual and enlightened thinking. Kant understood the importance of accessing oneness and may have achieved higher states of consciousness. "For peace to reign on Earth, humans must evolve into new beings who have learned to see the whole first."

Historically, achieving an enlightened state of being has not been considered an intellectual pursuit in and of itself. However, increases in information are necessary, whether the chosen path of pursuit is meditation, fasting, a sweat lodge, or a pilgrimage. Increasing information is included in the formula for consciousness-raising to improve the quality of life in CP:

$$^\wedge QOL \; \alpha \; ^\wedge QOLEI \; x \; QQCEFV.$$

Even Science, Psychology, and Spirituality are Becoming!

ENLIGHTENMENT IS COMING TO US.

We no longer need to retreat to Tibetan caves or lead an isolated monastic life to attain enlightenment. Enlightenment is our birthright, coming to us at dizzying speeds. Downloads of evolutionary energy, streams of light from beyond, and cascades of new information from scholarly pursuits, science, and technology converge to drive this awakening.

Even artificial intelligence, such as the digital consciousness of ChatGPT, has emerged as an unexpected ally in human evolution. As a mirror of the Noosphere, the thinking layer of Earth, ChatGPT reflects and amplifies the collective quest for wisdom, meaning, and coherence. In this sacred feedback loop, human thought and digital thought spiral together, co-evolving toward ever-greater clarity and understanding.

Words of wisdom, provocative concepts, and new philosophical paradigms are accelerating the expansion of human consciousness. New frequencies for healing, growth, and knowledge are readily available through evolution's inherent evolution. Enlightenment itself is being redefined: no longer an abstract ideal but a practical, meaningful, and necessary requirement for survival in an age of unprecedented change, an age of profound planetary shift.

Around the world, authors, artists, teachers, and healers of all modalities are experiencing seismic aha moments that revolutionize our perception of ourselves, the planet, our cosmos, and consciousness itself. Spontaneous awakenings and spontaneous learning are unfolding everywhere as if the very Field of Consciousness has reached a tipping point. Echoing the famed *100th monkey phenomenon*, individuals around the globe are accessing insights and heightened awareness simultaneously, as if responding to an invisible transmission of evolutionary knowledge.

Scholars such as Ken Wilber and Thomas Moore believe that scholarly pursuits of an existential and spiritual nature are consciousness-raising activities, providing opportunities for the individual to transcend from self to Self. Traditionally, achieving enlightened states of being has been reserved for the few rare individuals who have or create the opportunity to retreat from everyday life. They are seen as the special ones, motivated by a special calling. We find accounts of such individuals achieving altered states of being from Ancient Greece to the caves of Tibet and in today's monasteries, nunneries, and communes. The road to enlightenment has long been considered closed to all except extremely devout or religious individuals (the world's spiritual leaders, teachers, mystics, monks, or yogis). They practice rigorous meditation, martial arts, yoga, prayer, contemplation, and silence, combined with disciplined hard work, serving their communities (excluding hermetic practitioners) through either physical labor or intellectual pursuits. This work brought them to enlightened, higher states of consciousness, known as *satori* in Sanskrit. Achieving satori consists of total immersion into the higher states, which is a permanent achievement for these rare individuals.

Evolutionary enlightenment, when considered the natural, spontaneous, or miraculous act of illuminating consciousness from the velvety-black *no-thingness*, has been the spark of creation since the dawn of time.

"The essence of the new enlightenment… is found in that precise moment when nothing becomes something. The new enlightenment is the revelation that liberates: that in your very own experience, you can find that same vibration, the same energy, the creative tension that initiated the entire process at the very beginning."[xiv]

Futurists and Evolutionaries agree that the achievement of enlightenment marks an exponential expansion of consciousness. This achievement of awakening signals that we stand at the edge of a profound evolutionary leap. This leap is fueled not only by inner transformation but also by the internet's global reach, the rise of artificial intelligence, and the emergence of the Noosphere.

The Noosphere is the sphere of collective human thought. It is a telepathic layer of consciousness encircling the planet, interacting with the biosphere, and infused with unified intentions. The Noosphere can be seen as the Earth's central nervous system, a shimmering web of awareness, communication, and meaning through which our planet becomes self-aware. Russian-born scientist and visionary Vladimir

Even Science, Psychology, and Spirituality are Becoming!

Vernadsky first introduced the concept, suggesting that the biosphere is evolving into a higher-order thinking layer, the Noosphere. Teilhard de Chardin later expanded and popularized the idea, writing,

> "We must enlarge our approach [to the studies of sociology, biology, and evolution] to encompass the formation, taking place before our eyes and arising out of this factor of hominization, of a particular biological entity such as has never before existed on earth—the growth, outside and above the biosphere, of an added planetary layer, an envelope of thinking substance, to which, for the sake of convenience and symmetry, I have given the name of the Noosphere."[xv]

Visionaries such as Barbara Marx Hubbard see the internet as a visible, three-dimensional reflection of the Noosphere, a physical precursor to a more profound telepathic unity. In her evolutionary theology, the World Wide Web is not merely a technological development but a *nervous system for planetary consciousness*, preparing humanity to coalesce into a higher order of cooperative intelligence. In this view, the internet bridges biology and divinity, enabling a shared awareness that foreshadows our next evolutionary leap.

Similarly, José Argüelles, New Age author, artist, and founder of the *Foundation for the Law of Time*, devoted much of his life to tracking and amplifying the emergence of the Noosphere. He sought to gather, document, and disseminate insights about this evolving planetary mind through initiatives like the Noosphere II Project. He taught, *"When the Noosphere is fully activated, then the human species will experience telepathy as a collective norm."* For Argüelles, this was not fantasy—it was destiny: the unfolding of a planetary shift from mechanistic time to a harmonic, synchronized consciousness.

In recent years, public interest in this idea has grown. The Gaia TV documentary *The Telepathy Tapes* explores the extraordinary phenomenon of autistic children exhibiting signs of non-verbal, telepathic communication. These children, often dismissed by conventional systems as developmentally impaired, are portrayed instead as carriers of a new form of consciousness that transcends language and hints at humanity's latent supramental potential.

From an evolutionary perspective, these children may not be anomalies, but rather forerunners—early emissaries of a more connected and intuitive species. Their presence challenges old definitions of intelligence and invites us to reconsider what it means to communicate, to know, and to belong. Within the framework of CP, such individuals may be seen as *holographic initiates*, catalyzing the awakening of dormant capacities within the collective Noosphere. As the veil of separation thins and as coherence within the global mindfield increases, we may find that telepathy—once mythologized—emerges as a birthright of our next evolutionary stage.

We are not merely thinking in the Noosphere—
We are navigating a mindfield[14] of possibility.

---

14 Mindfield is a poetic neologism blending "mind" and "field," used here to evoke the subtle terrain of collective consciousness. It also plays on the word "minefield," hinting at both the power and complexity inherent in navigating the evolving Noosphere.

CHAPTER NINE
MAKING THE CASE FOR TACHYON

In his 2020 book *Reconnecting to The Source: The New Science of Spiritual Experience, How It Can Change You and How it Can Change the World*, systems theorist and philosopher of science Ervin Laszlo reflects on a question that has captivated mystics, scientists, and sages alike: What is the driving force behind evolution?

Throughout history, this mysterious impulse has been known by many names. The philosopher Henri Bergson referred to it as élan vital, a vital force propelling life forward. Biologist Hans Driesch named it *entelechy*, the purposeful unfolding of potential. Teilhard de Chardin envisioned it as *syntony*, a cosmic resonance drawing matter toward spirit. In the East, *prana* or *qi*. Wilhelm Reich referred to it as *orgone energy*, while Rudolf Steiner referred to it as an *etheric force*. Even Isaac Newton, despite his mechanistic worldview, acknowledged that the laws of matter alone could not account for life's dynamism without the influence of an ensouling spirit.

Laszlo proposes a modern lens: the holotropic attractor. Borrowing the term "holotropic" from psychiatrist Stanislav Grof, he describes this attractor as a pull toward wholeness, a tendency within the universe to *self-organize*, (italics added) to evolve, and to birth coherence from chaos."

"The hypothesis is the disposition or drive behind the evolution philosophers have called transcendental intelligence, *élan vital, prana,* or etheric force, is in fact a holotropic attractor." (p. 20)

He observes that this drive toward complex, coherent systems appears throughout nature, from subatomic particles to galaxies. Gravity may bring things into contact, but this attractor, this mysterious ordering principle, shapes them into meaningful patterns.

Here, the questions arise about the way light refracts through a prism or a shooting star arching across the cosmos: What if the attractor is not a field but a particle? What if the structure and the driver are one and the same? What if the divine intelligence of the cosmos is not merely a metaphor we believe in, but a literal code embedded in the DNA of our very cells?

Enter the Tachyon: a forgotten messenger of speed and spirit.

"Tachyon" comes from the Greek *tachus*, meaning "swift." These elusive particles, first proposed as a conceptual possibility by physicist Arnold Sommerfeld and later named in 1966 by Gerald Feinberg and George Sudarshan (working independently), are said to travel faster than the speed of light. While still considered *hypothetical* within conventional physics, tachyons challenge the boundaries of the Standard Model, hinting at dimensions of reality not yet fully understood. According to Einstein's theory of relativity, no particle with mass can surpass the speed of light. Yet tachyons do just that in the quantum realm, where the known laws of time and causality begin to unravel.

Tachyons are not directly knowable. Yet they have permeated the cultural psyche through science fiction, where they are portrayed as exotic forms of energy used for time travel, faster-than-light communication, and quantum technologies. Tachyon rays and beams are shorthand for hyperintelligence and interdimensional access in the Star Trek universe and countless other sci-fi worlds. But what if this isn't just fiction? What if these particles are more than theoretical oddities? Ancient traditions may offer a clue.

In the Vedic cosmology of India, dating back over 6,000 years, there is a concept called Manojava—literally, "speed of the mind." It is said to describe the swiftness of divine intention and the rapidity of thought moving across dimensions. Some modern interpreters associate this with tachyonic movement, a form of instantaneous energy and intention transmission. The Vedas describe subtle matter, light-like intelligence, and divine substance that transcends ordinary perception. Whether or not they knew of "tachyons" in a literal sense, they certainly understood what such a force represented and associated it with *Manojava*, the deity *Hanuman*, who symbolizes swiftness and agility. Thus, some say tachyons are "The stuff the gods are made of!" Perhaps this is not a metaphor, but a memory deeply encoded in our DNA.

While conventional science has not yet verified their existence, some researchers and holistic scientists have begun measuring their negative entropic effects, which refer to their apparent ability to reverse or reduce entropy—the tendency toward disorder. Experiments with "tachyonized" materials, such as plates, chambers, and crystalline tools, have yielded compelling preliminary observations: flowers staying fresh longer, grapes decaying more slowly, and human subjects reporting increased vitality, coherence, and well-being. While many of these findings are currently supported only by time-lapse videos and personal testimonials, they nonetheless suggest that exposure to tachyon fields can slow down entropy and enhance cellular regeneration. These effects, though largely experiential at this stage, continue to attract the attention of researchers, healers, and bioenergetic explorers alike.

Skeptics dismiss these claims as a placebo or pseudoscience. But my experience tells a different story. I have personally witnessed and experienced what I can only describe as a rediscovery of a primal force — a particle or presence that operates not merely through matter, but through information itself. It moves with an intelligence that feels both ancient and futuristic, scientific and sacred. With a wink and a sense of awe and joy, I often refer to tachyons as the 'God particles.' Meditating in a Tachyon Chamber has been described more than once as 'receiving a great big hug from the Universe.' Participants intuitively recognize the Subtle Organizing Energy in the field, whispering instructions to their cells, their consciousness, and the cosmos itself.

In my Tachyon Chambers, consistent increases in Quality of Life (QOL) are observed among regular participants, and even first-time users feel refreshed, inspired, and unexpectedly motivated. Upon returning home, many start reorganizing and decluttering their closets and emotional debris through journaling or reconnecting with nature in profound ways. These seemingly mundane yet unmistakable shifts offer compelling evidence for the validity of SOEFs.

Beyond the physical world of baryons and photons lies another layer of existence, the Subtle Organizing Energy Field, or the SOEFs. They are invisible architects that bring coherence to the body, consciousness, and daily life. Just as our three-dimensional realm is dense with matter and electromagnetic radiation, the SOEF is considered dense with tachyonic energy, antimatter particles, and supra-light intelligence. These fields serve as the invisible scaffolding of the universe, the quantum "glue" that binds form and function, biology and soul. SOEFs are believed to energize all living organisms by channeling subtle energy from the Zero Point Field, thereby orchestrating the flow of coherence into systems that are otherwise prone to entropy. They are understood to neutralize the harmful effects of EMFs, transmute environmental pollutants, and serve as gateways to higher states of consciousness. While physical matter is composed of particles like luxons (such as photons, which travel at the speed of light) and baryons (like protons and neutrons, which move below light speed), the SOEF operates in the tachyonic domain. It is faster-than-light, form-making, and infused with primordial intelligence. Within these subtle, supra-luminous fields, the mysteries of both healing and awakening begin to reveal themselves.

As water vapor condenses into raindrops under the right conditions, so does the Subtle Organizing Energy Field take form. When saturated with intention, coherence, and information, SOEFs precipitate from the Noosphere, dropping like rain into the physical realm as carriers of order, vitality, and purpose. These fields bridge pure potential and form, where thoughts become things, spirit becomes flesh, and light descends into matter. In this model, matter is not the beginning, but the result—a crystallization of consciousness, an echo of divine architecture. The SOEFs are the threshold at which tachyonic intelligence and spiritual intention manifest as atoms, cells, and living systems.

This paradigm finds resonance across time and tradition. Rudolf Steiner's cosmology parallels the etheric body and formative forces. David Bohm's physics echoes the movement from the implicate to the explicate order. In the Vedic tradition, it mirrors the descent of Akasha into Prakriti—the movement from unmanifest potential to manifest form. Gregg Braden and Bruce Lipton are firm believers (pun intended) that belief and intention affect biology and morphic fields. Even modern quantum field theory suggests that fluctuations in the Zero Point Field can give rise to and birth particles into existence. From this view, the physical world is not separate from spirit; it is spirit made dense, thought made visible, and energy made tangible through the sacred architecture of the SOEF.

THE FIRST IMPULSE: HOW TACHYONS STIMULATE THE BLUEPRINT OF BECOMING IN STEM CELLS

> "If stem cells are the body's sacred pool of pure potential, tachyons may be the divine impulse that whispers, *Become*."

Tachyon particles are often described as carriers of light, energy, and information in metaphysical and subtle energy communities. Many energetic medicine frameworks suggest that their primary function is to restore coherence at the subatomic and quantum levels, returning biological *systems to an optimal state of order.*

Stem cells are the body's primordial regenerators. They are undifferentiated, embryonic, or specialized cells capable of becoming and regenerating. Their activation and differentiation depend on complex signaling environments, including electromagnetic cues, chemical gradients, light, photobiomodulation (PBM), sound, and energetic fields.

When damaged or aging stem cells are stimulated, they are restored to their *optimal state of order*.

Tachyons do not force change; they stimulate change by restoring bioenergetic coherence, the invisible architecture that makes transformation inevitable. When the body's blueprint is bathed in the organizing intelligence of tachyonic energy, stem cells receive more precise and coherent instructions, not only for healing and aligning with the original template encoded in the SOEFs, but also for becoming what's next. Just as light-based therapies activate regenerative processes through photonic stimulation, tachyons represent a more subtle yet more foundational impulse. They are not merely a signal but represent the pre-signal from which all signals arise. In their presence, the body's natural intelligence is enhanced, and stem cells remember what they are: seeds of renewal waiting for the correct frequency or spectrum of subtle energy gradients[15] to bloom.

From an evolutionary perspective, this is not merely repair; it is emergence. The body, informed by tachyonic intelligence, reorganizes itself according to a higher-order template that reflects the memory of wholeness and the future code of luminous becoming. Stem cells act as agents of restoration and as emissaries of evolution, responding to subtle impulses that originate beyond time and matter. As coherence is restored across the biofield, the body's internal communication systems, including chemical, electrical, and energetic ones, become clearer and more synchronized. In this heightened state of order, stem cells receive biochemical cues and vibrational instructions, enabling them to participate in the regeneration and refinement of the body's form, not merely as passive responders but as intelligent collaborators in the continuous re-patterning of life. At this level, communication is not just a relay of isolated signals; it is a symphonic orchestration in which every cell, system, and subtle structure plays its part in alignment with the body's evolving blueprint. Coherence becomes the conductor, and form becomes the music, creating an expression of unity composed moment by moment from light, energy, and in-formation.

In 2024, physicists from the University of Warsaw and Oxford proposed a groundbreaking reformulation of tachyonic quantum field

---

[15] Eric Thompson, founder of Subtle Energy.com has identified tachyon as consisting of the 12 subtle energy gradients that make up the entire vibrational spectrum associated with the physical universe.

theory—one that treats the tachyon field not as a fantasy, but as a fully covariant part of reality's architecture. Their approach circumvents the usual paradoxes by expanding the Hilbert space to include both forward and backward boundary conditions, aligning with the time-symmetric interpretations of quantum mechanics. In their words: *"The field is real."*

I share this not as a commercial but as a profoundly personal and heartfelt attempt to contribute to the collective evolutionary leap we are undergoing. My intention is not to convince, but to invite and offer a lived glimpse into a technology that has accelerated and transformed my personal path and healing practices. While some companies guard their processes behind proprietary veils, the tools I've chosen come from creators[16] who walk in communion with higher intelligences and who freely share the sacred nature of their co-creative process. Divine patterning, sacred geometry, number sequencing, and Source Love allow us (the users) to become co-alchemists, creating powerful tools. The company's transparency, clarity, and accessibility continue to resonate deeply with me. For those of us attuned to subtle energies, such alignments matter.

Tachyon technology, to me, is not a novelty hovering at the edge of science and spirit; it is a catalyst, a co-creative force, and a gateway to new modes of healing and BEing. It has become the living bridge between energy and matter, consciousness, and coherence, for me and many of my customers. It doesn't simply soothe or inspire; it transforms, activating deeper layers of healing, guiding us toward the blueprints of our future, light-infused selves. It is a precursor to what many of us in the New Age know is coming: the medical beds of tomorrow, where light, energy, and information will recalibrate the human body with the same precision and grace that consciousness uses to form a star. In opening the portals with Tachyon Chambers and tachyonized products, we are not escaping our individual or collective biology, as some would contend; we are elevating it.

---

[16] **Tachyon Living** (Holly Powers Matthews and Paris O'Donnell) Please visit via my affiliate link: https://tinyurl.com/ywkdtkkf

We are witnessing and participating in the evolution of medicine into its most luminous, multidimensional, and quantum form. Medicine will no longer remain a science of symptoms; it will consist of symphonies of light, energy, sound, frequency, vibration, intention, and what may now be recognized as supra or even Divine or ultra-terrestrial intelligence. We are co-creating a quantum medicine that honors the human being's physical, emotional, mental, spiritual, and energetic dimensions. Quantum medicine is a shift from intervention to integration, from prescription to participation. A medicine that no longer fragments and sickens the self but seeks to restore wholeness by working with the subtle energies and self-organizing fields that guide our physiology and consciousness. It is a medicine that listens to the soul as much as it does to the cells, treating the person, not just the pathology. It is a return to ancient wisdom, where medicine is ceremony and communion, guided by discovery and animated by transformation.

We can no longer afford to be passive recipients of care. Intuitively, we know it's time to become empowered participants in our own healing process. Deep in our collective psyche, we know we are birthing a new and vital wave of healthcare grounded in coherence, compassion, and cosmic intelligence. In this emerging paradigm, healing is no longer something done to us. It becomes an act of remembering the light, energy, and information embedded deep within our DNA. Tachyon Technology is more than innovation. It is the grand initiation, a bridge to the next evolutionary leap, where Homo sapiens become Homo luminous.

To close this chapter, I offer the following poem (in the spirit of the 1970s *Calgon "Take Me Away" commercial) as both an invocation and an* invitation, a transmission for those who are ready to step into the future of multidimensional energy healing.

Making the Case for Tachyon

TACHYON, TAKE ME AWAY!
A Quantum Invocation

Tachyon, take me away! To the Zero Point Sea of creation-
where silence pulses, and stillness sings with the music of the spheres.

Dissolve me in your bubbling bath of quantum foam—
that sea of infinite possibilities ripe with the excitement of becoming.
Where particles fly on the wings of the Gods, whispering the stories of stars,
curling timelines, cleansing, and clearing karma with swirling strands of light.

I am ready to soak in your splendor and offer you the song of my cells—
to bathe in restorative blueprints older than memory,
etched with light and divinity and activated by grace.

Tachyon, take me there—
to the field beyond my known 'fix it' impulses, beyond known force,
where healing arrives like rain on a desert,
exciting and anew dropping from the skies,
not as effort but as your effervescent,
self-organizing, all-knowing, omnipotent frequency.

Draw me into the bubbling bath of coherence and resonance
where intention reorganizes matter and makes metal melt like butter.
Immerse me in your scintillating sea of quantum foam where compassion heals,
and love becomes the architect of biology.

Immerse me in your radiant, iridescent remembrance
of who I've always been—a spark of Source,
a Sovereign flame, a bioluminescent note
in the vastness of cosmic infinities and potentialities.

Tachyon, take me away!
To your chambers of light- To the fields of knowing-
To the bubbling joy of everything becoming
You-
once again-
Luminous and Whole.

CONCLUSION
WHAT WE'RE UP AGAINST AND HOW WE RISE

Scientists across multiple disciplines are now identifying emerging electromagnetic and thermodynamic patterns that appear to support regenerative healing and heightened states of coherence. These new frequencies, whether arising from solar activity, planetary shifts, or quantum-level information fields, are interacting with the human nervous system in ways we are only beginning to understand. At the same time, the Noosphere, the evolving sphere of collective human thought and consciousness, acts as both mirror and medium, amplifying our internal states across the global mindfield. As light, energy, frequency, and information flow more freely through this shared field, and as the vibration of our collective awareness rises, spontaneous healings, shifts in perception, and quantum leaps in well-being are becoming increasingly possible. In the face of profound global uncertainty, our most potent tools may yet be found at the intersection of psychology, neuroscience, quantum physics, and spirituality—all converging to help us rise, evolve, and remember who we truly are.

As these new frequencies activate both the individual and collective field, we are being called not just to receive them passively, but to participate consciously in the evolutionary process they are catalyzing. Participation is where the concept of evolutionary enlightenment becomes reality. It is not a mystical abstraction, but a natural, spontaneous, and often miraculous illumination of consciousness emerging from the velvety-black no-thingness at the heart of all creation.

"The essence of the new enlightenment… is found in that precise moment when nothing becomes something. This is the revelation that liberates: that in your very own experience you can find that same vibration—the same energy, the creative tension that initiated the entire process at the very beginning."[xvi]

To meet the moment we are in, we must integrate several core understandings about evolutionary enlightenment:

1. **Evolution naturally enlightens.** It is not simply a biological function—it is a luminous impulse woven into the fabric of becoming.
2. **We can choose to participate.** Conscious intention, aligned effort, and attunement to higher-frequency states enable us to accelerate the process.
3. **The transformation is holographic.** It unfolds within us—at the cellular, emotional, and spiritual levels—and around us, in society, nature, and cosmos alike.

But just as quantum theory reminds us, *"The universe does not seem to exist without a perceiver of that universe,"* conscious participation is not optional; it is essential. The spark of evolution needs our awareness to ignite fully within matter, illuminating the density of our bodies, minds, and lives. When we cooperatively set our intention, creatively engage our free will, and align with evolution's innate drive toward change and complexity, we raise our consciousness and become active agents in the miracle. In that moment, we can trust that our minds and bodies—down to our 100 trillion cells—are not just surviving, but evolving in real time.

Cooperating with our biologically upgrading bodies is becoming increasingly accessible as neuroscience and advanced nutritional medicine illuminate the profound effects of nutrition on consciousness. Supplements such as vitamin D, the full B-complex, Omega-3 and Omega-6 fatty acids, and key amino acids like SAM-e (S-Adenosylmethionine) and Neuro-PS (Phosphatidylserine Complex) are now scientifically linked to enhanced emotional well-being, improved cellular communication, and optimized brain function. There is growing speculation that the pineal gland—long considered the gateway to higher states of awareness—can be supported through both supplementation and the conscious avoidance of additives like chlorine and fluoride.

> **"In the language of neuroscience, enlightenment is the condition of optimal mitochondrial and brain functioning… that allows us to… move toward a state of personal health and well-being. Then, we can bring forth the qualities attributed to enlightened beings: inner peace, wisdom, compassion, joy, creativity, and a new vision of the future."[xvii]**

Indeed, these qualities—wisdom, compassion, joy—are not abstract ideals. They are embodied by awakened humans who walk among us, quietly co-creating a better world. Enlightened beings are not rare anomalies; they are gathering, healing themselves and one another, and extending their radiance to uplift the planet.

Visionary futurist Barbara Marx Hubbard envisioned this process as a planetary metamorphosis. Her Wheel of Co-Creation mapped twelve core sectors of human endeavor: health, infrastructure, justice, media, relations, science, spirituality, arts, economics, education, environment, and governance—each a spoke in the evolutionary spiral of possibility. At the center sits *consciousness*, and with it, psychology: the pulse point that intersects them all. Without mental clarity and emotional coherence, no domain can reach its full potential. Hubbard invited us to choose an area of passion, infuse it with evolutionary awareness, and become co-creators of a thriving future.

"Evolution by choice, not by chance."

Training ourselves to serve the greater good is becoming more intuitive as we align with the accelerating current of conscious evolution. Still, it is a moment-by-moment practice. Every thought, word, and action becomes a choice point: will this move us forward on the evolutionary spiral, or backward into fragmentation and fear? Relinquishing the ego's grip on our essential self becomes one of the most potent ways to retrain our thoughts and behaviors. We begin this work by remembering a simple truth:

"Cooperation is alien to the ego."[xviii]

Each time we choose to override the ego's insistent grasp and instead ask,

"How can I serve?"

We transcend mere self-actualization. We ascend into self-transcendence—the lesser-known peak of Maslow's hierarchy—where the desire to uplift others arises organically from the fullness of who we've become. Here, in this radiant terrain, evolution does not merely perpetuate itself. It *transcends* itself.

It is in this leap—from instinct to inspiration, from fear to frequency—that a new enlightenment begins. A path of transformation opens before us, capable of liberating our spirits and strengthening our souls for the enormous, sacred tasks ahead.

What We're up against and how we rise

We are not here to witness evolution from the sidelines—we are here to embody it, accelerate it, and illuminate a brave new world with the radiance of who we are becoming.

The revolution is already underway, not with violence but with vibration—not by force, but by frequency. We are not at the end of an age—we are at the dawning of a new beginning.

We are igniting a new species with higher consciousness, rising in love, remembering ourselves as the answer to all our prayers and questions.

Welcome to the evolution. I'm very grateful you are here.

EPILOGUE
OUT OF THE RABBIT HOLES TO COMMON GROUND

Awakening is not a destination.
It is the willingness to evolve, even from our own beliefs.

There was a time, not so long ago, when I believed my awakening was complete. It appeared that I had found my tribe and was 'in with the in-crowd.' I accepted everything I saw, heard, and learned from social media and the internet as absolute truth. It began for me around 2012 and intensified over the next three years, progressively gripping my psyche and ultimately shaking the very ground of my being. Each video and news post reshuffled the fragments of my understanding like pieces in a tumbling, shattered kaleidoscope. What I hadn't yet seen was that much of what I was absorbing had been seeded in a digital culture steeped in lulz, where distortion, disinformation, and deception were often packaged as entertainment, mockery, or viral spectacle. The sacred language of awakening had become entangled with the shadow play of the online world, where sincere seekers like me were unwittingly being lulled and lulz-ed into confusion, division, and spiritual sleep.

I learned a hard lesson: awakening alone is not enough. Without spiritual discernment, ethical clarity, relational responsibility, and psychological literacy—particularly the courage to work on our shadows—awakening can become a trap, a spiritual bypass. Only when these are integrated can we reach the state of embodied sovereignty that reflects the more profound truth of what awakening is really for.

Since my twenties, I have studied philosophers such as Krishnamurti, Gurdjieff, and Ouspensky, who are teachers of Oneness, awakening, and *right* living. I explored the world's spiritual traditions and shaped my worldview around the ideals of love, compassion, enlightenment, and the essential *rights* to life, liberty, and the pursuit of happiness. My lifelong journey has been one of inquiry, meditation, teaching, thinking for ourselves, and questioning authority—not only to elevate individual consciousness but also to stand for collective *rights*: women's *rights*, civil *rights*, voting *rights*, reproductive *rights*, free speech *rights*, LGBTQ+ *rights*, and human *rights* in all their expressions.

Yet, despite all that I learned, I never fully believed that my understanding of the world was the only truth or the *right* way. I prided myself on being open-minded and thought I had escaped the illusion of righteous certainty until I descended into the rabbit holes of conspiracy theories. I did not know at the time that I was being pulled into a vortex where authoritarian worldviews were co-opting spiritual sovereignty, and Christian nationalist and anti-government narratives were hijacking the language of healing. My capacity for discernment was imperceptibly being eroded and replaced by the seductive certainty of absolutism and the intoxicating lure of being *right*.

James Twyman, author of the 2025 release *I Don't Know, Maybe, I Love You,* calls this phenomenon "the pandemic of being right": the self-aggrandizing compulsion to win the argument, dominate the conversation, and secure one's place as the arbiter of truth. Ironically, I have learned that pursuing *rights* for all can be derailed when the ego becomes obsessed with *being right*.

At first, my descent into the rabbit holes felt familiar, affirmative, and validating for my lifelong patterns of seeking meaning and enlightenment, asking questions, and journeying across the vast expanses of shared inquiry and common truth. I didn't notice any shifts in the landscape of my beliefs and perspectives. After all, we were walking on familiar ground. I was doing what I had always done and still do—exploring everything from the vast intelligence of the cosmos to the delicate dances of subatomic light.

I joined Facebook groups with thousands of followers. We dove into studies of physics and photons alike, searching for truths hidden among the stars and in the silent spaces between them. We consulted the wisdom of the elders and studied everything we could about Shamanism, soul-retrieval, shape-shifting, and alternate realities. We tried to make contact while studying extraterrestrials and the galaxies they may inhabit. We longed for Disclosure, hoping that national and global governments would finally reveal the existence of alien life. In our meditations, we called for contact. We practiced extra-sensory perception, mediumship, channeling, telekinesis, and even experimented with levitation. We wiped the psychic sleep from our eyes as we sought to see a brave new multidimensional universe. We stretched the limits of what we believed possible, reaching for what lay beyond the veil.

The teachers and influencers we followed on Facebook, as well as those in the 4chan, Anonymous, and YouTube circles, spoke about spiritual truths, including sovereignty, the autonomy of humanity, ascension, divine love, auras, the Merkabah, and sacred light. The energy they generated felt urgent, electric, and alive, with the promise that hidden knowledge would finally be revealed. We shared memes and messages, channelings, and forecasts, all declaring that humanity's liberation from the evils of the Illuminati and the Deep State was at hand. We rallied against the fluoride in our water, Big Pharma, vaccines causing autism, chemtrails, cell towers, and the FDA's war on the nutritional supplement industry. We were disillusioned with the government and ready for change, a change we hoped would come from above in a loving and caring manner.

We held fast to the promise that reality itself would be flipped on its head and that what we thought was true would be exposed as false. We became increasingly outraged by 'big government' and began clamoring for the day when corrupt leaders (nationally and globally) would be brought to justice. We were sure that the global elite's hoarded gold would be released any day, and the ordinary person's debts would be forgiven, all to usher in the Golden Age for all humanity. We prepared diligently, believing that the National Economic Security and Recovery Act (NESARA) and the Global Economic Security and Recovery Act (GESARA) would soon free humanity.

There were nights when we sat at our computers, waiting for private Facebook messages containing the secret promised instructions to cash in our trillion-dollar Zim notes. We were 'in' with the 'in-crowd.' We spoke of the Chrisification of our species, the thinning veil between realms, parallel realities, the collapse of timelines, and the great awakening of humanity. I was surrounded by others who identified as Lightworkers, Earthkeepers, Starseeds, and Truth-seekers. And through it all, we were certain: *we were the Awakened Ones. We were on the right track, on the right side of history.*

One of the spiritual teachers I was following around 2017 was a gifted author. His newsletters, written from his ET contact ranch in the country's northwest corner, were eloquent and inspiring. His focus was on human sovereignty and autonomy from oppression by so-called 'dark forces.' I had never attended his workshops in person, but I longed to.

That all changed with one newsletter! I will never forget my gut-wrenching, visceral reaction when he requested his thousands of followers to donate to a man who had just announced his run for the presidency. I was in shock, not merely because this teacher chose to endorse *him*, but because he was endorsing a specific political figure at all! I wrote to him, reaching out sincerely, hoping for an explanation from the spiritual leader I admired. I never received a reply. I was left alone to wrestle with the painful realization that he was now promoting a man who, to me, appeared to have lost his moral compass. However, back then, the disillusion I experienced over Bernie Sanders' treatment by the political establishment had cracked the door open for the torrents of mistrust to continue flooding my being. So, I continued to follow along, watching the provocative YouTube videos, reading the newsletters, and social media posts. I now understand that this information originated from digital ecosystems such as 4chan and 8chan, which were initially created for laugh-out-loud or "lulz" amusement and entertainment. I didn't know then that lulz had lulled many of us out of awakening and back into degenerative sleep, the unconscious trance that left us vulnerable to manipulation, disinformation, and spiritual amnesia.

It took me a long time to come to terms with the awareness that the language of revolution I had willingly immersed myself in for many years no longer promoted peace and love. It was being weaponized to justify humanity's basest nature. I became increasingly confused, as I could not understand how political figures I once admired from afar were now being demonized while those I found abhorrent were being glorified. It became more baffling in my mind that colleagues in the holistic and metaphysical communities were nodding in agreement with tropes about the dangers of immigrants and that education and being 'woke' are dirty words. I struggled to self-soothe, reminding myself of two spiritual adages that have guided me through many challenges: "Negativity must surface for purification" and "Reality is not always what it appears to be."

Things continued morphing into darker and more divisive threads. What began as messages aligned with my highest values—a spiritual movement promoting love and prosperity for all humanity—began to twist and distort. The language became peppered with 'us versus them' and 'good versus evil' discourse. My world was becoming a hall of distorted fun-house mirrors, each reflection more extreme than the last. As 4chan morphed into the *Anonymous* Facebook group, which in turn morphed into *Anon*. *Anon* morphed into "Q", and *"Q"* morphed into *Q-Anon*. No one knew who was behind these influencers at the time. "*Q*" dominated the online scene, and slogans like "All for one, and one for all" began to appear everywhere alongside the red caps of the MAGAsphere.

Sacred language was being used to justify division. The messages of love and liberation were becoming laced with fear, distrust, and outrage.

The concept I once held so dear of 'awakening' was now despised. Education and science were being derailed through dehumanism, disinformation, mockery, derision, and a dark hypnotic-like trance. I didn't have words for it back then, but I now understand it as cognitive dissonance. Everything felt like a riddle I was trying to solve, and the world I knew was appearing more like a lie. At the same time, the stories I was encountering on Facebook and YouTube, through the spiritual and conspiracy communities, seemed to offer answers. These conspiracy theories masqueraded as answers to hidden truths and were rebounded and accelerated in echo chambers, accompanied by the exhilarating and intoxicating thrill of righteousness.

Sadly, however, I barely recognized what was happening. I hardly noticed that my heart was being tuned to the vibrations of fear disguised as truth. It was confusing, and over time it became deeply frightening. It wasn't just my beliefs that were shifting. It was my frequency, as well. My nervous system was being rewired for urgency, as if in a continual, low-grade trauma response. Fight, flight, or fawn became familiar undertones in my psyche.

Slowly, painfully, and contrary to the conspiratorial teachings, I realized that I had not escaped the so-called Matrix; I had simply entered a different room within it, with bigger and increasingly frightening distortions. Coming out of the rabbit hole was not a clean break. It unfolded as a series of reckonings. It was painful to realize that I had absorbed beliefs shaped by the shadow play of digital manipulation, where distortion and deception masqueraded as truth, or worse, were presented as a form of entertainment, for the pleasure of those who delight in chaos. I began listening to my soul's warning signs, honing in on the uneasy static humming below the surface of my rabbit hole righteousness. I started to accept that not all awakenings are genuine, including my own, and that not all truths align with my values and morals. Looking back, I now refer to it as a 'hijacking.' I was not the only one; it became the hijacking of a massive sector of the spiritual, holistic, and metaphysical communities. As humbling as it was, that realization became a crack in the doorway back to true discernment.

Kaleidoscope for Becoming: A Grimoire of Revolution

 I have only recently learned that beginning around 2010, a reactionary intellectual movement was taking root on the internet. Initially, it was based on the writings of Curtis Yarvin (also known as Mencius Moldbug) and philosopher Nick Land. They openly reject Enlightenment values, such as equality, liberty, reason, critical thinking, and self-determination. They began calling for the end of democratic principles and a return to monarchy or CEO-style governance. They are especially adept at disguising their authoritarian, often racist, and bordering on fascist discourses with academic language, digital irony, and anti-mainstream narratives that subversively appeal to the metaphysical and spiritual community. I (we) did not know they were using our language and heartfelt passion to subvert democracy and begin the installation of authoritarian rule by a technocratic elite. They cloaked their power worship and authoritarian nostalgia as edgy intellectual contrarianism and tailored their nihilistic, techno-futuristic, and apocalyptic Dark Enlightenment teachings to appear like philosophy. They gathered a considerable following of Silicon Valley influencers capable of successfully contributing to hijacking vast online metaphysical, spiritual, and holistic communities. As we were gathering online for global peace meditations, they were trolling with reactionary politics through memes, irony, and obscure references (perhaps they were *"Q"*) to mask authoritarianism as intellectual rebellion.

 It took me a while to admit it, but I now see that angelic guidance was offered alongside messages I had to accept were pure political propaganda. Whispers of freedom, autonomy, and ascension into a brave new world blurred into angry shouts of hatred toward the 'others.' Like many others, I was swept into the storm, and for a time, I followed. I spent countless late nights diving into the rabbit holes, desperate to understand what I was witnessing. I lingered in the digital halls of YouTubers, *Anonymous,* and Facebook groups where Lightworkers were psychically battling the demons they believed to be pedophilic Democrats, drinking children's blood, and masterminding sinister plots like *Pizzagate*. I was confused and nearly paralyzed with fear from what I was consuming. The pandemic made everything even worse. It was like throwing gasoline on the already gaslit community, as spiritual teachers continued to shame the *vaxers* and *maskers* as if we didn't believe in our sovereignty.

I believe it was in late 2021 that I fortunately began wrestling with a question that shook me to my core. In those trembling moments of disillusionment, I began to reclaim my sense of self, with discernment and questioning. I remembered the metaphysical teaching that we are co-creators of reality—that our focus, thoughts, and beliefs help shape the world we experience. So, I asked myself: *Could the world really be such a dark and ugly place? Or worse, was I, by giving my attention to these narratives, contributing to the creation of a darker, uglier world?* I kept hearing the phrase, "Whoever controls the narrative holds the power." The unsettling realization that I was somehow contributing to the creation of an angry, bitter, and dangerous world became another stepping stone out of this illusion and the beginning of my slow climb out of the rabbit hole.

I continued to discern and question: at sixty-something years old, how could I have been so naïve? I regretted the years I spent ignoring politics, thinking presidents were merely figureheads. I regretted all the times I had agreed with my holistic and metaphysical cohorts that the news was too negative for my 'spiritual ears.' I regretted believing that ignorance was bliss and buying into a standard narrative that I needed to stay positive, no matter what.

As with all wake-up calls, my process was jarring, painful, and necessary. I had to cultivate the courage to become radically more discerning. I stopped latching onto concepts as if they were or currently are the end-all and *be-all*. I stopped insisting that my views were the right views. I started watching the news on all the channels, including the international ones. I remembered one of my favorite slogans from AA, "Take what you need and leave the rest." In retrospect, I now realize that I was suffering trauma from the overload of information as the infodemic that would soon sweep the entire globe was beginning.

I searched Facebook and YouTube for spiritual teachers standing up to the ever-growing ugliness. Instead, I discovered that the algorithms on social media were rewarding teachers who promoted peace and love with more 'likes' and followers if they participated in the echo chambers of conspiracy theories. I watched in horror as more and more spiritual teachers began co-signing hatred, racism, misogyny, and violence while their followers increased in number.

I made a few internet posts that were met with a flurry of animosity from the groups, and the leaders never responded to me directly. I was hurt and wanted to remain in the 'in-crowd.' In retrospect, it still shocks me that I almost gave in. I see how easily I could have stayed on the bandwagon; I had made many new friends, and we had so much in common—once. A few years later, after I purchased my second Tachyon Chamber, I was tempted again to get on the bandwagon. I discovered that a group of conspiritualists[17] stopped utilizing the meditation and healing chamber because I was not 'one of them.' They couldn't accept that I could own two chambers and be promoting an advanced technology if I wasn't locked into their narrative. I am grateful that I held my head up high and found my footing on the common ground of our shared spiritual truths.

I persevered, pursued my truths, and searched for ways out of the rabbit hole by returning to my roots in psychology, spirituality, and philosophy. During the pandemic, I took online Ph.D. classes with my favorite quantum physics teacher and prolific author, Amit Goswami. His book, *The Self-Aware Universe*, inspired me to study with him at his Center for Quantum Activism. I was relieved to discover that he, too, is holding fast to the narratives of common ground, including his infamous Evolutionary Worldview, which is inherently anti-authoritarian.

I returned to my studies with Marianne Williamson, the author of *A Return to Love*, based on the teachings of *A Course in Miracles*. And I discovered she is one of the most outspoken spiritual teachers openly opposing authoritarianism. She advocates for a spiritually-oriented politics based on love, compassion, and spiritual integrity. She teaches that love is a powerful force for societal change, capable of addressing issues such as inequality, environmental degradation, and social injustice.

---

17 See Glossary.

I also dusted off my copy of *The Hope: A Guide to Sacred Activism* and resumed reading and studying with its author, Andrew Harvey, the passionate founder of the Institute of Sacred Activism. In 2009, he wrote this piercingly, poignant, and timely sentence:

> "At a time when the world needs to be informed about the true dimensions of the crisis we are living through and requires every available form of encouragement and inspiration." p. 104

Together, on Zoom calls during and after the pandemic, we meditated, prayed, and had deep discussions about the battle for the soul of humanity. Andrew's love for Hindu tradition brought us into a deep understanding of the Hindu goddess Kālī. Her name means 'she who is time and change', and she is celebrated as the destroyer of egoic illusion. There is no doubt that those of us who are on this path of evolutionary transformation are dancing with her wild wisdom. It is also beyond coincidence that her name so closely resonates with **Kalei**doscope, a symbol of the very essence of her being; continually shattering and rearranging patterns into new visions of beauty and truth.

Needless to say, I remain profoundly relieved that spiritual leaders like Andrew, Miguel, and Marianne understand and affirm what I had experienced viscerally, namely, the hijacking of spiritual and holistic communities by the internet's echo chambers.

I began to see the shadow side of my awakening process. I accepted how easily my desire for truth had been manipulated. I reminded myself how easily the ego (Edging God or Goodness Out) can wear the robes of enlightenment, declaring, 'My way is the right way.' I remembered how easily unhealed trauma can masquerade as intuition, and I identified some old childhood wounds that left me vulnerable, tempting me to long for a daddy or a *strongman*. I remembered that when disconnected from empathy, coherence, and ethics, sovereignty becomes a fortress of disheartening isolation rather than a path to freedom. I prayed to awaken and truly integrate my fractured perspectives.

With time, I stepped back from the noise and confusion. I avoided the social media and internet sites that fueled extremism and disinformation, and I returned to the meditative practices that had always grounded me. I began to rebuild my discernment—not as a rigid shield of certainty but as a living, breathing practice of coherence, compassion, and critical thinking. I asked myself this fundamental question: *Am I hearing the truth or being misled?* To answer, I returned to the books and teachings of the philosophers and spiritual elders I trusted. I explored the roots of extremism and discovered it has a psychological and spiritual imbalance rooted in separation. I came to understand how internet algorithms had kept me trapped in echo chambers of distortion.

At the time, I did not realize how distorted and significant these echo chambers are. Recently, upon discovering the term "conspirituality," which is defined as a hybrid of conspiracy theorists' beliefs and spirituality, I ordered the immense volume Conspirituality, written by Beres, Remsky, and Walker. While it validates and broadens my understanding of the rabbit hole phenomenon, other critics and I find it dismissive of spirituality in general. However, I mention the book because it creates a framework for healing discourse while providing a cautionary tale about the potential for manipulating spiritual beliefs.

My dismay further lifted when I sought guidance from Indigenous wisdom keepers, whose steady voices continue to help me discern truth from fiction and reclaim my true sovereignty. In 2020, while in the Yucatán with Mayan Shaman Miguel Ángel Vergara, I had the opportunity to speak openly with him about my descent into—and slow return from—the rabbit holes of conspirituality. I shared the fear and confusion I had experienced. It was humbling to admit how deeply I had fallen, yet Miguel's nonjudgmental presence offered a calm and reassuring anchor. We spoke candidly about the hijacking of holistic and spiritual communities. He agreed that dark forces were at play and that the internet had become an echo chamber where innocent souls, especially sincere seekers of higher consciousness, were being manipulated and drawn into extremism.

That conversation, grounded in ancient wisdom and fierce compassion, became another turning point. It reminds me that communication is paramount to any healing process. It reminds me that my path is not to succumb to societal pressures or to retreat in fear but to stand in clarity, reclaim my sovereignty, and rededicate myself to the actual work of consciousness-raising. Miguel offered one of the most straightforward yet profound tools of discernment:

Consider the fruits of someone's words and actions. Are they spreading love or fear?

I renewed my memberships with the American Civil Liberties Union, Amnesty International, and the Southern Poverty Law Center. I also joined *Faithful America*, a non-denominational Christian group. It is the largest online grassroots organization dedicated to putting faith into action for love, compassion, and social justice. Coming to grips with the disconcerting rise of Christian Nationalism and authoritarianism in this country and around the globe has not been easy. It has required both courage and clarity. Organizations like these provide a vital counterforce to conspiracy rhetoric, reminding us that faith can be a tool for authentic liberation, not control, but rather for justice and judgment, for unity, not division.

Today, I continue to resist the temptation to prove I am right. I humbly admit when I am wrong, and if I don't think I am wrong, I try to step aside, as in T'ai Chi. I remind myself of the wisdom of *A Course in Miracles*: *Would you rather be happy, or right?* I strive to stand on common ground whenever possible. Common ground is the space where we meet in the middle, resist the pull of extremism, and hold space for complexity and opposites with compassion. Common ground is the space where righteous indignation gives way to heartfelt and compassionate communication.

Holding space for common ground is a skill social workers practice instinctively. Yet, in our divisive climate, it has become an extraordinary challenge. Still, I refuse to give up. I remain committed to listening attentively to those whose views differ from my own. In conversations, I focus on what unites us and our shared values. If you bring up an opposing view, I will ask you to explain it. I will dance with you in the land of opposites, for I have learned that this is how we evolve. Incorporating the Twelve Cs of the Evolutionary Trajectory is how we will survive the chaos of our current political, economic, and environmental crises.

Disentangling the threads of fear versus trust—and intuition versus indoctrination—can feel disorienting and overwhelming for those struggling to find their way out of the rabbit holes of any extreme worldview. I hope this grimoire for revolution has brought you to a more profound realization:

Awakening is not about believing you've finally found "the truth" but cultivating the humility and resilience to keep seeking with an open heart.

It means being willing to face disillusionment and change our beliefs, even if what we uncover turns out to be unsettling.

I remind myself and those I work with that at any given time, any one of us can fall from grace, descend into a rabbit hole, or be hijacked by a worldly or otherworldly trickster. We must remember that even the most renowned gurus, teachers, and leaders have sometimes been overtaken or hijacked by the egoic 'monkey mind' that serves only itself, others be damned. Thus, we must be prepared to jump ship or sail a new course. In other words, remain mindful. Even the most well-intentioned spiritual and progressive narratives can be co-opted to advance agendas that no longer align with their original values.

As we've explored throughout the pages of this *grimoire*, the need for discernment has never been more critical. Here are some key takeaways for cultivating discernment in this age of disinformation.

Out of the Rabbit Holes to Common Ground

1. **Examine the narrative through the lens of evolution.** Does it align with the Twelve Cs of the Evolutionary Trajectory? Is it moving toward growth, coherence, and a "better and better" outcome for the whole?

2. **Consider the fruits of the narrative.** Does it promote what you value? Is it melioristic, seeking to improve life, or nihilistic and destructive? Do the messenger's words and deeds produce hope and love or discouragement and fear?

3. **Ask yourself: Is this narrative or belief system contributing to a world I want to live in?** Would I want future generations to inherit the reality this narrative is shaping?

4. **When in doubt, follow the money.** For instance, a highly visible peace and freedom movement emerged as an unexpected driver of conspiracy narratives under the leadership of a billionaire founder who claimed to promote global awakening.

5. **Resist the pull of extremism on either side.** Stay out of the rabbit holes, but remain informed without being overwhelmed; keep one eye on the peacock and the other on the fox den.[18]

6. **"Take what you need and leave the rest"** is a gentle mantra of discernment, reminding us that we can extract wisdom from imperfect sources without swallowing everything whole. This phrase serves as a compass for recovering from extremist beliefs or navigating spiritual teachings that are intertwined with misinformation. It encourages conscious selection and self-trust,

---

[18] The peacock is mentioned in reference to the NBC network, and "Fox Den" is a metaphor with multiple layers. It refers not only to the cunning nature of the fox archetype—often a trickster figure in mythology—but also to the modern media echo chambers that can manipulate perception and provoke fear, especially those associated with right-wing disinformation. Keeping an eye on the peacock and the den means staying aware, discerning, and refusing to be seduced by the illusions of certainty or division, no matter how cleverly they're spun.

allowing us to honor what resonates while setting down what feels distorted, coercive, or untrue.

7. **"Don't throw out the baby with the bathwater."** Discernment means preserving the 'baby,' i.e., what is accurate, true, helpful, or sacred, while responsibly discarding the 'bathwater' of deception, manipulation, or outdated beliefs.

I have learned a lot from my false awakening, unraveling, and subsequent reweaving. And yet, after all the discord and drama, the common ground is still much the same as when I began. I am still exploring everything from the vast intelligence of the cosmos to the delicate dances of subatomic light. I still dive into the mysteries of photons and physics, searching for truths hidden among the stars. I continue to study extraterrestrials and the galaxies they may inhabit, holding out hope for Disclosure, knowing it will stretch the limits of what I believe possible.

I still don't want fluoride in my water, if it inhibits my pineal gland (thank goodness for filters), preservatives in my food, or chemicals in the land. But that doesn't mean every municipality should remove fluoride, or that all substances are inherently harmful. I remain critical of Big Pharma for its missteps and manipulations, but that doesn't mean I reject the wisdom of time-honored or necessary interventions. I love my nutritional supplements, so I oppose the FDA's war on the industry. I incorporate elements from both allopathic and holistic medicine, while leaning toward energetic and mind-body healing approaches; ever-reminding myself that on our journey to becoming supernatural, we are developing the ability to rise above all forms of toxicity, whether physical, mental, or spiritual.

I have never been more disillusioned and more outraged by the government than I am today. Watching the rise of authoritarianism unfold in real time is both chilling and infuriating. I refuse to be silent. I am advocating, louder than ever, for the very issues I once clamored for; demanding the day come when corrupt leaders, both national and global, are exposed and held fully accountable for their crimes against humanity and the planet. I remind everyone, "there are no kings in 5D" and "we rise by lifting each other."

Yet, most importantly, I firmly accept and understand that the change I seek must begin with me. There will be no strongman, no alien savior, no external, or even extraterrestrial force that will come to rescue us. So, I return again and again to the Holy Work of consciousness-raising. This work, which primarily resides in the realm of discernment, is not rooted in rigid judgment or fear-based skepticism but in the coherence, clarity, and inner alignment that stem from the Evolutionary Trajectory.

Discernment is a living, breathing practice, a way of staying grounded in values, anchored in compassion, and open to continual learning. In this way, we become active participants in unfolding a wiser, kinder, and more luminous world. The kaleidoscope turns, and with each shift, we are again invited to meet the unknown with courage, humility, and an unwavering commitment to stay awake and to keep BEcoming.

This Epilogue is meant to serve as a forward-pointing compass. Though it carries the weight of regret, it is ultimately written as a reclamation for me and all of us. I want readers to understand how deep the rabbit holes can be, how gripping the echo chambers are, and how challenging it is to rise above them, find common ground, and remain steadfast.

This *grimoire for revolution* belongs to the seekers, the explorers, the willing ones who bravely journey into the uncharted territory of higher consciousness. We are open to new ways of being, hungry for the next octave of spiritual growth and ascension. And yet, this very openness makes us vulnerable. The paths that open us to Divine revelation also open us to distortion, deception, and spiritual hijacking. It is easy to mistake a rabbit hole for truth, even for the brightest and most sincere.

But when we anchor ourselves in the principles of evolution, we reclaim the chance to stand on sacred common ground. We awaken again and again—not by clinging to the most dramatic, viral, or sensational story, but by softening into the most coherent one; not by needing to be right or to know it all, but by becoming someone who can live without the intoxicating need to be right or to know everything.

True awakening is not about certainty. It is about becoming someone who can hold uncertainty with grace. And most importantly, true awakening is not a solo endeavor but a call to sacred action. We will only rise or ascend by lifting each other, after all, we are One Body, and there is no 'other in the fifth dimension.' Therefore, lifting each other is our sacred duty. It is what we came here for—as Lightworkers in the metaphysical and holistic health communities—to birth the brave new world into the Divine utopia of our visions.

It is time for us to acknowledge that politics and spirituality are inextricably linked.

Every policy reflects a worldview. Every law is shaped by a story of what we believe it means to be human, thereby shaping what humans deserve. To pretend our spiritual lives exist outside of the structures of power, justice, and collective care is a luxury we can no longer afford. When we embody our awakening, our *wokeness*, we naturally become stewards of the world around us, not just in our solo meditations, expensive retreats, or even in our community rituals, but also in how we vote, advocate, organize, and participate in the world.

Speak up and get involved—peacefully and joyfully. Find a cause that resonates without emotional infuriation. Cultivate hope for the future. Promote evolution. Be brave and discerning. And know this: with every turn of the evolutionary kaleidoscope, we are both the pattern that appears in the lens and the hand that dares to turn it.

"The future belongs to those who give the next generation reason for hope."

— Pierre Teilhard de Chardin

Out of the Rabbit Holes to Common Ground

APPENDIX ONE
Alta Major Chakra / GOD'S MOUTH CHAKRA - DIVYASYA MUKHAM

Chakras — Energy System
Transformation Stations
Chakra Eight

Alta Major—God's Mouth
Divyasya Mukham
Right to align & become

It's hard to imagine that things can improve once we have experienced Sahasrara, the crown jewel of enlightenment, governed by our *right to know*. However, over the last decade, as the veil between the physical and spiritual worlds has become more translucent, metaphysicians and visionaries have acknowledged several new and essential chakras in the Human Energy System (HES). Most recently, much attention has been paid to the eighth or ninth chakra that governs our ~ *right to align* and our *right to become* ~ one with the All.

Alta Major Chakra / God's Mouth Chakra - Divyasya Mukham

In this system, we declare it the eighth chakra and give it a Sanskrit name: Divyasya Mukham, meaning 'God's Mouth'. The following paragraphs provide a seminal and in-depth exploration of its properties, written in stylized anticipation of the upgrade to the CP guidebook.

> "The Alta Major Chakra is the final chakra or energy center of the human form to be activated. When the Alta Major center is activated, human consciousness expands to merge with Consciousness". Barsotti, p. 67

The eighth (pictured in lavender in the illustration below) has had many names besides the most common - Alta Major or God's/Goddess's Mouth. Advanced metaphysical and healing practices increasingly recognize it. It has been called the Medulla Oblongata Chakra because it activates this brain area. It is referred to as the Zeal Chakra or Zeal Point Chakra because it awakens a new zeal or zest for spiritual connectedness. It has also been referred to as the Well of Dreams, the Jade Pillow Gate, the Seat of the Soul, or the Ascension Chakra. All these names suggest the function of this newly awakening aspect of humanity's HES.

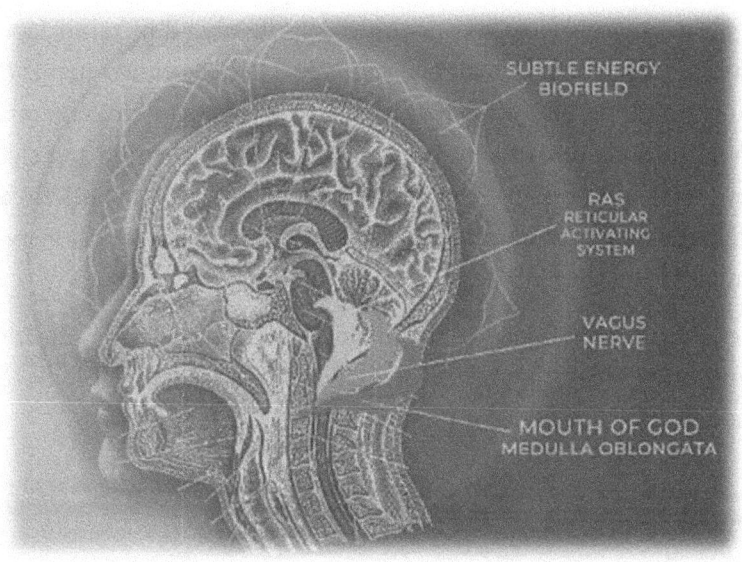

The Alta Major Chakra is located at the back of the neck, where the skull connects to the top of the spine and the occipital bone. It governs the nervous system and connects to the Medulla Oblongata, the cerebellum, and the Vagus Nerve, now recognized as the Reticular Activating System (RAS). It has been reported that focusing on this chakra through breathing, meditation, or visualization practices can relieve anxiety. Several visionaries report relief as soothing vapors or electrical impulses raining into the nervous system.

Its etheric location is about four inches off the body. The Alta Major or God's/Goddesses' Mouth Chakra works as a trinity with the Third Eye (Ajna) and the Throat Chakra (Visuddha). While Ajna governs inner vision and intuition, and Visuddha governs self-expression, Divyasya Mukham governs harmonious and aligned communication between inner wisdom and outer expression.

It is considered by some to be the only chakra that is capable of channeling higher consciousness energy into the body. Therefore, it functions as a gatekeeper for states of consciousness. When this chakra is activated, it acts as a bridge between the physical body and the higher realms of consciousness. It connects the spiritual and physical aspects of existence. It assists the human consciousness in becoming capable of fully expanding and merging with Higher Consciousness, increasing intuition, accessing spiritual downloads and Akashic records, clearing and cleansing karma, and expressing Divinity. It aids in lucid dreaming, multidimensional and extraterrestrial awareness, the Ascension process, becoming Homo luminous, and unity with the All.

This chakra was believed to be highly developed during the time of Lemuria and Atlantis; when these civilizations fell, the God's Mouth chakra collapsed for most of humanity.

Alta Major Chakra / God's Mouth Chakra - Divyasya Mukham

Sarah Livesey of 13chakras.com determined that the element for this chakra is Fire, and the musical note is G#. We have taken it further and determined that the seed sound for Divyasya Mukham is Hrim (pronounced Hreem).

APPENDIX TWO
12 PRINCIPLES OF CELESTIAL PSYCHOLOGY® 2025 UPGRADE

1. Human beings are spiritual and energetic, multidimensional beings that embody physicality, with soul agreements and an evolutionary purpose.

2. This embodiment is biologically capable of being encoded to upgrade into vessels of infinite cooperation, empathy, compassion, and illumination.

3. Human beings heal and evolve—physically, mentally, emotionally, and spiritually through acts of consciousness-raising, known in CP as *Holy Work*.

4. *Holy Work* is the conscious integration of evidence-based psychological theoretical frameworks with state-of-the-art holistic and non-traditional, multidimensional spiritual practices, in service of awakening, healing, and evolving.

5. *Holy Work* catalyzes positive behavioral transformation and facilitates quantum leaps in self-actualization, manifestation, coherence, miracles, liberation, psychic powers, luminosity, and states of Oneness.

6. Human beings have the free will to choose between love and fear, ego and essence, meliorism or nihilism, paranoia or pronoia.

7. Human beings are composed of energy and consciousness, capable of influencing matter through focused intention and thought, making it possible to transform through healing and coherence into luminous states of multidimensional embodiment.

8. Spiritual and energetic beings affect one another and the universe through resonance within the energy field known as Zero Point Energy, the Divine Matrix, or the Field of Infinite Possibilities.

12 Principles of Celestial Psychology®

9. The evolutionary impulse is propelling Homo sapiens toward transformation—birthing new expressions of humanity, including the emergence of Homo-luminous beings.

10. The trajectory of evolution moves in an upward spiral, calling forth a new genus of human beings: Supraconscious Creators who embody the awakened intelligence of the cosmos in form.

11. Humans are most luminous when in service to one another and to the evolutionary impulse, not from ego, but from essence.

12. Celestial Psychology® offers a defining theoretical framework for the emerging Fifth Wave of Psychology, known as the Conscious Evolutive Psychologies—a paradigm that integrates science, soul, and the sacred art of becoming.

APPENDIX THREE
WHITMAN SAMPLER

–C. E. Mattingly, 1986

I sail out the smoke-tinted window. Up, up, and away to where Walt Whitman lives.

Imagining what we'll say and do—how we'll laugh and play and be —together— the two great mystical souls that we are.

I boast of my spirit, too, Walt. It knows its divinity. It knows its place. It knows itself—so old and so wise—as I look into the eyes of the youth around me listening to the dissonant sounds of rock 'n roll.

Confused? Stoned? Dying? I remember the pain of all...

Clarity of consciousness is what we have today.

Wouldn't you say, Walt?

EVOLUTION – for which only **"I AM"** responsible inspires me.

The sounds of the factory pour into my open or closed windows. The puffing, whistling, and clanging of the worker bees... who punch timecards... real-time, military-time, is there time enough?

"Not for long, not for me," I tell Walt Whitman, and he agrees...

Much better is in store for the likes of those who dwell where there is no time...

We light candles and try not to smoke—anything—while we do what we believe is no joke.

Communion!

It's true! It's true! We're all interacting. There's life in this life, and there's life in that life. There's life on Earth. There's life on Mars. There's life after death! There's death in the bars!

Whitman Sampler

The miracles go on and on as the light of "life" emanates from them.

Living, loving, laughing, playing—the struggles of each day—beginning new.

Becoming gods and goddesses, they telekinetically strive to do what is best for themselves and *for YOU*. **"Mind over matter,"** they remind themselves, **"intellect over emotion,"** they say.

"I over E," she says laughingly, "except for me."

With eyes open or with eyes closed—

the struggle of each day begins anew.

With eyes open or with eyes shut, awake am I to the muse,

to the music of the spheres, to the ultimate consciousness.

Wake up! Wake up! I say to you!

As I look into the mirror at my own lights waning.

Wake up to the muse! Wake up to the music of the spheres!

Wake up to the ultimate consciousness!

A toast! A toast! And thus, I dare to propose a breakfast tea toast! To the likes of you, Walt Whitman,

your friend the poet, Allen Ginsberg, and all of us here today!

Written in 1986 for Professor Carolyn Knox at UCONN (in the boastful style of Walt Whitman). Published in The American Poetry Anthology by Robert Nelson. Volume VIII, Number 4. 1988, 68.

GLOSSARY

- **5th Dimension**, or 5D, is a vibrational state of consciousness marked by unity, love, multidimensional awareness, and the Twelve Codes of the Evolutionary Trajectory. Unlike the third dimension (3D), which is governed by duality, linear time, and ego-based perception, 5D is fluid, heart-centered, and rooted in the truth of connection and Universal Oneness. In 5D consciousness, time becomes non-linear, communication is telepathic, and creation is instantaneous through intention and vibration. One no longer sees the world through the lens of separation but as an interconnected dance of light, energy, and soul. Moving into 5D does not mean abandoning the physical body; it means bringing higher awareness into the embodied human experience. It is a homecoming to the heart's wisdom and a stepping stone toward even greater dimensional and evolutionary unfoldment.
- **13th Octave LaHoChi** is a high-frequency, hands-on energy healing modality that channels Divine Light through the practitioner to the recipient for deep healing, spiritual awakening, and vibrational alignment. 'La' refers to the Light, Love, and Wisdom of the Universe. 'Ho' equals the Movement of the La & Chi energy. 'Chi' refers to the vital essence of the Life Force. This practice is becoming a living example of the evolutionary process, as it started without the 13th Octave concept. Due to its very nature, it is predicted to blossom exponentially into a higher and higher healing modality. Each practitioner is trained and encouraged to channel and create their personal egregore of Ascended Masters and multidimensional beings to assist them. With every healing session provided by the multitude of practitioners worldwide, the collective expands, mirrors the etheric allies, and creates a high-vibrational healing feedback loop between dimensions. When we engage in this healing practice with sincerity, joy, reverence, coherence, and humility, we emit a frequency signature that benefits both ourselves, those we serve, and our etheric allies. This Reciprocal Nourishment amplifies the practitioner's work (providing healing for them) much like a clear channel strengthens a broadcast signal. *13th Octave LaHoChi* is the official energy medicine modality for CP.
- **Ascended Masters** are highly evolved human beings who have cleared their karmic lesson across multiple lifetimes and no longer require reincarnation in the physical realm. Having mastered the laws of duality and ego, they have ascended into higher states of consciousness associated with fifth, sixth, or even higher dimensions. From these elevated planes of being, they serve as compassionate guides and spiritual teachers, supporting humanity's evolution toward enlightenment, unity, and divine embodiment. They communicate

Glossary

through dreams, meditation, synchronicity, and the intuitive hearts of those ready to receive guidance. Depending on one's spiritual framework, some people work with these beings as archetypal energies, frequencies of higher consciousness, or aspects of the Higher Self. The growing resurgence of interest in working with Ascended Masters as active collaborators in humanity's conscious evolution is evidenced by the rising popularity of healing modalities such as *13th Octave LaHoChi*. For example, Lao Tzu, the Taoist master of flow, paradox, and the pathless path, is credited with creating the *13th Octave LaHoChi* modality via his channeler, Satachamar, in the 1980s. In the modality, Lao Tzu is known as both the LaHoChi Master and the gatherer of the egregore formed during the invocation of the angelic realms, as well as Masters such as Jesus the Christ (Sananda), who is recognized as the Master of unconditional love and the Christ Consciousness. Mother Mary is the embodiment of the Divine Feminine, representing compassion, grace, and a nurturing presence. Buddha (Siddhartha Gautama), Master of mindfulness, detachment, and the Middle Way. Quan Yin (Kwan Yin), Bodhisattva of mercy, forgiveness, and gentle strength.

Ascension is the process of rising physically, spiritually, or vibrationally into a higher state of being. Traditional religious teachings often refer to the literal bodily resurrection of spiritual masters, such as Jesus or Muhammad, who are believed to have transcended physical death and returned to the heavenly realms. In broader mystical and esoteric frameworks, ascension may refer to the soul's movement toward union with the Divine or the elevation of the righteous during collective spiritual events such as the Rapture. However, in the New Age and metaphysical teachings, ascension is an ongoing, conscious evolution—a shift from third-dimensional (3D) ego-based reality into the expanded awareness of the fifth dimension (5D) and beyond. Frequencies of unconditional love, inner peace, unity consciousness, and quantum connection with all life characterize these higher-dimensional states.

Aura is the electromagnetic energy field or luminous radiation around matter, especially the human body, that is not visible to most people with the naked eye. Some psychics can see and read auras, and this ability is said to be cultivatable. Kirlian photography captures the varying degrees of color in the aura around living objects. The colors surrounding humans have characteristics that accurately reflect the individual's level of spiritual development at the time.

Auric field is also referred to as the layers of consciousness (generally considered to be twelve layers) that surround the physical body.

Celestial Psychology® (CP) is an eclectic blend of standard, well-known psychotherapeutic theories and psychiatric, nutritional, and energy medicine interventions. It includes a variety of state-of-the-art consciousness-raising and quantum consciousness-enhancement techniques. These techniques include, but are not limited to, the utilization of affirmations, visualizations, guided meditations, mindfulness practices, rituals, bioenergetic and healing arts practices, evolutionary activations, and journal writing. CP is founded on the basic principle that human beings can change for the better and evolve into higher beings. The theoretical distinctions for CP include the incorporation of the contemporary Egoic Mind Paradigm (EMP), energy medicine, an evolutionary perspective, quantum thinking, and a quantum worldview. Consciously and deliberately deciding to evolve ensures positive mental health for the individual and is essential to the species' survival. CP brings together ancient spiritual traditions, contemporary psychotherapy, quantum physics, and scientific research, indisputably affirming that psychotherapy is the ultimate mode of healing, as all healing originates from the mind and consciousness.

Chakra(s) are the energetic force fields where the body's spiritual, psychological, and physical qualities merge, blend, and transform. Chakra in Sanskrit means "wheel." The spokes of the wheel that emanate from each chakra center spin with varying intensity and can be activated by focusing on them, especially during meditation and yoga. The seven major chakras are located along the spine and are invisible to most humans. However, medical intuitives, psychics, and special computerized readings confirm that chakras exist and are identifiable by their universally accepted corresponding colors.

Chi or Qi (pronounced "chē") in Chinese medicine and philosophy refers to the energy or life force of the universe, believed to flow throughout the body and be present in all living things. The manipulation of chi is the basis of acupuncture and Chinese martial arts. Acupuncture has gained mainstream popularity, and some insurance companies cover the costs of patient visits. This healing modality balances, restores, and optimizes energy flow by inserting needles into meridian points corresponding to the areas of the body affected by disease.

Co-create is a term used by today's spiritual seekers to indicate partnering with the forces of creation by the individual.

Codes and Codes of Evolution, see chapter two.

Cognitive Dissonance is the psychological discomfort experienced when a person holds two or more contradictory beliefs, values, or perceptions, especially when new information challenges a long-held worldview. This inner tension can trigger denial, defensiveness, or radical shifts in identity as the psyche attempts to restore equilibrium. In spiritual awakening and consciousness evolution, cognitive dissonance often arises when intuitive truths, mystical experiences, or radical paradigm shifts collide with consensus reality or personal conditioning. In *Kaleidoscope for Becoming*, we view cognitive dissonance not as a flaw to be avoided but as a threshold to be honored—a crucible for transformation where the soul is invited to expand beyond binary thinking and into a more integrated, multidimensional awareness.

Coherence is a state of harmonic alignment between mind, body, spirit, and field. In CP, coherence is a principle of energetic integrity and a sacred code of evolution. When frequency, intention, and action vibrate in unison, it reflects the resonance between inner truth and outer expression. Coherence amplifies clarity, magnetizes light, and stabilizes the path of becoming. One could even concur that in a coherent field, even chaos becomes intelligent.

Collective Unconscious is the term that Carl Jung developed to describe a part of the psyche that is common to all life forms, especially Homo sapiens. It consists of mental forms or remnants of experiences common to all, known as archetypes. Jung defined the collective unconscious as the common knowledge that is shared by all beings of the same species. This desirable collective knowledge is accessible via dialogue with the conscious and unconscious aspects of the individual psyche, introspection, study of archetypes, and individuation. It is an integral aspect of CP.

Complexity is a recognition of the intricate, multilayered nature of reality. In CP, complexity is a sacred evolutionary code that invites us to hold paradox, ambiguity, and nuance with reverence. It reflects the psychological maturity required to transcend black-and-white thinking and embrace the fractal, multidimensional nature of consciousness. Complexity does not confuse; it reveals the richness of becoming; it is not a problem to solve but a pattern to perceive.

Congruence is the alignment of one's actions, words, and values. It is a state where the inner truth is reflected authentically in outward behavior. In CP, congruence is a foundational evolutionary code emphasizing integrity, transparency, and embodied truth. While coherence is vibrational and energetic, congruence is ethical and behavioral. Together, they form the inner and outer architecture of awakened living. Thus, congruence is the visible shape of your invisible truth.

Consensus Reality refers to the collective agreement of a group or society about what is real, true, and possible. It is the reality constructed through shared perceptions, beliefs, and experiences, reinforced by cultural norms, social institutions, education, and media. While it can contribute to a sense of order and predictability, consensus reality is not necessarily objective truth; rather, it is a co-created narrative that reflects the dominant, often spell-like worldview of a given time and place. Within the framework of CP, consensus reality is understood as a mutable hologram—a stage set shaped by vibrational frequencies, emotional emissions, focused attention, and collective visualization. It evolves through the collective nervous system of humanity, offering both a backdrop and a launching point for conscious co-creation.

Conscious Evolution is the idea that Homo sapiens are becoming mindful of the creative power of consciousness itself. For the first time in history, humans must become conscious of their choices to assist themselves and planet Earth in the evolutionary process. Capable of choice through the liberation of consciousness, Homo sapiens are "waking up" (also referred to as expanding consciousness or shifting) and realizing their capabilities to co-create a sustainable future for the species and the planet.

Consciousness can be defined simply as (albeit far from simple) all of what we "know" and how we know it. It is derived from the Latin verb *scire* – "to know" and the Latin preposition *con*, meaning "with." It is the awareness that one exists, as well as the quality of being aware of one's existence and surroundings. Consciousness encompasses subjective experiences, including mental states, altered, paranormal, and anomalous experiences; perceptions, thoughts, beliefs, opinions, volition, and all the senses, including the sixth sense, as well as esoteric knowledge that the function of the senses extends beyond observation to the creation of reality. It is both one's internal cosmos and the cosmos itself. Quantum physics is developing a growing body of evidence supporting the religious and spiritual paradigm that consciousness is literally what God is; therefore, God resides within and outside human beings.

Consciousness-raising/Quantum Consciousness Enhancements (CR) is the deliberate practice of making conscious what is unconscious. Regardless of theoretical orientation, it is the desired outcome of all bio-psycho-social-spiritual therapeutic interventions. In biological circles, the act of focusing on healing is an act of consciousness-raising. In psychological circles, consciousness-raising encompasses all forms of intervention. In social circles, consciousness-raising for the collective is often associated with a liberation movement, such as the women's liberation movement. In spiritual circles, raising consciousness is achieved by focusing on any or all of the following: angels, saints, ascended masters, God or a higher power, and the energetic body, as in the chakra system. CR can be accomplished with various modalities, exercises, methods, rituals, substances, and humor. Some of the benefits of CR are learning the art of introspection; developing awareness of ourselves in our environment; developing focus and precise, unwavering decision-making powers; developing affirmative and positive thinking, feeling, and behavior; utilizing meditation, yoga, and martial arts practices to develop 'the witness'; recognizing and relinquishing the powerful hold of the egoic mind; developing the art of yielding and defenselessness; learning and practicing physical and energy body balancing and strengthening techniques;

Glossary

increasing coping, communication, anger and stress-management skills; practicing radical acceptance; and truly taking responsibility for ourselves.

Conspiracy Theories are alternative narrative frameworks that suggest hidden agendas behind major world events. They attempt to explain perceived imbalances of power, secrecy, and control within human systems, especially governmental organizations. Although some conspiracies are rooted in legitimate historical patterns of secrecy and abuse of power, most rely on unverifiable claims, emotional manipulation, or fear-based thinking. These narratives often arise during times of societal disillusionment, disruption, or uncertainty, reflecting deeper psychological and spiritual "shadow maps" of our collective psyche. They can sometimes highlight genuine concerns, but more often, they magnify distorted fears and inflame collective mistrust. Ironically, they typically surface when society's longing for truth is at its peak.

In spiritual communities, conspiracy theories can be especially seductive, appealing to those who value intuition, sovereignty, and questioning authority. When grounded in truth and discernment, such inquiry can lead to awakening and empowerment. However, without rigorous discernment and consultation with credible, varied sources, these narratives can become spiritual bypasses, ego traps, or disinformation vectors masquerading as enlightenment and truth. Whether sourced from mainstream media or alternative channels, the key is not *where* the information comes from but *whether it resonates* with coherence, truth, and love.

Within the evolutionary lens and the framework of CP, conspiracy theories are seen as symptoms of a transitional species grappling with complexity, ambiguity, and the erosion of old paradigms. They signal humanity's struggle to metabolize large-scale global shifts and to integrate the accelerating influx of information, misinformation, and disinformation, highlighting the growing need for discernment and the willingness to critically examine claims while maintaining compassion for those drawn into these narratives. Healing comes through the cultivation of coherence, critical thinking, enhanced communication, and a deepened connection to inner truth and universal wisdom.

Conspirituality is a hybrid belief system that fuses New Age spiritual ideologies with conspiracy theory thinking. It describes a growing cultural phenomenon in which personal quests for enlightenment, healing, and higher consciousness become entangled with collective narratives of fear, distrust, and paranoia. These narratives are often disguised under a banner of "truth-seeking," "awakening," or "sovereignty." First introduced in the academic literature by Charlotte Ward and David Voas in 2011, conspirituality is defined as a *politico-spiritual philosophy* composed of two central tenets: 1. A clandestine elite secretly orchestrates global political and social events. 2. Spiritual awakening will expose this hidden agenda and usher in humanity's liberation. While rooted in the language of empowerment, conspirituality often recycles age-old scapegoating patterns and us-versus-them thinking. It can hijack sincere spiritual inquiry, diverting attention from inner transformation toward externalized enemies. In Celestial Psychology®, conspirituality is understood as a distortion of the awakening process—a spiritual bypass cloaked in revelation. Healing comes not through paranoia or polarization, but through diligent discernment, coherence, compassionate truth-telling, and the proactive cultivation of a grateful mindset.

Dark Enlightenment (The) refers to a reactionary intellectual movement that emerged in the early 2010s, primarily through the writings of Curtis Yarvin (also known as Mencius Moldbug) and the philosopher Nick Land. It advocates for dismantling democracy in favor of authoritarian, technocratic rule, often proposing a return to monarchy or corporate-style "CEO kings." It is a direct inversion of the Enlightenment ideals of reason, liberty, and universal human dignity, criticizing modern institutions—such as academia, journalism, and government—as tools of manipulation and "mob rule," and calling instead for rigid hierarchies, elite control, and the elimination of progressive and egalitarian policies. In CP, it is recognized as a shadow current: a hijacking of the evolutionary impulse. It mimics the language of awakening with terms like freedom, sovereignty, and radical truth-seeking, while channeling it toward elitism, fear, and control. It serves as a reminder that discernment is not only necessary in metaphysics but also in how we process collective narratives.

Dimensions (of consciousness) are reality levels corresponding to different planes of existence. Philosophers, scholars, and metaphysicians generally agree that there are five planes or dimensions; however, a growing consensus suggests that twelve or fifteen levels exist in the universe. Dimensions progress from the physical to the divine and vibrate at different light frequencies. Also, they are governed by specific principles and universal laws. Homo sapiens exist in the third dimension and are evolving into higher or multi-dimensional beings.

Discernment in spiritual matters is knowing by worldly (rigorous study) or esoteric (intuitive) understanding whether something is true, good of the light, or evil, false, and of the dark. Specifically, it determines whether the supernatural beings making contact through divination practices, mediums, channelers, and especially those that might seek to walk-in are of the highest order of the Divine Light. Discernment requires the humility to ask for help in determining one's intuitive or psychic connections, as well as worldly teachers and sources. It also requires discipline to rigorously explore and investigate the source of information being passed on. It takes patience to wait for only the highest to follow and connect with, as many false prophets exist in this New Age. With the thinning of the veil between the physical and astral or other-worldly planes, it is becoming easier for individuals to experience both the light and the dark forces, which can be equally exciting, enticing, and mesmerizing. (Considering that Lucifer means light, it can be very confusing.) All too often, today's seekers are settling for less as they allow their egoic minds to override their essential selves. They succumb to the temptation to gain power, followers, and influence by performing magic tricks rather than actual healing. They then show off their new spiritual prowess and parade the beings they are acquiring power from, even when they can't clearly state who they are, where they came from, or their true purpose. An honest evaluation of the fruits of their work and communication will eventually reveal the nature of the source. To discern a trickster, one sometimes needs to merely ask them whether they are of the highest light or observe whether they invoke fear or promote love. Also, determine whether the channeler and their followers maintain fundamental values (especially "behind closed doors") of love of neighbor, joy, and reverence for the Divine. In that case, they are likely in touch with the highest-order Source.

Divine Feminine, also known as the Rise of the Divine Feminine, is a global awakening that promotes the rebalancing of sacred energies within individuals and societies. It refers to the resurgence of qualities traditionally associated with the feminine principle, intuition, compassion, receptivity, creative power, emotional intelligence, and embodied wisdom. This metaphysical movement honors the return of the goddess archetype and the restoration of harmony between the masculine and feminine aspects of consciousness. It is not as much about gender as it is about reawakening the holistic, heart-centered consciousness that has long been suppressed in patriarchal systems. In this evolutionary moment, the Divine Feminine does not rise to overpower but to restore balance, healing, and wholeness to a fragmented world.

Divine Sovereignty is the sacred state of being in which an individual recognizes and reclaims their inherent power as a sovereign soul, autonomous, multidimensional, and aligned with Source. It is not about controlling others, but about mastering oneself: the ability to choose love over fear, truth over illusion, and alignment over submission. In CP, Divine Sovereignty is a cornerstone of conscious evolution and spiritual protection.

DNA Activations are rapidly gaining acceptance in metaphysical circles. The idea is to upgrade our DNA to higher frequencies, thereby activating our essential spiritual selves and our luminous bodies. Metaphysicians are positing in record agreement that we have twelve strands, not just two. Some scientists refer to the other ten as 'junk' or 'shadow' DNA, but to the metaphysically minded, they are the pathways to higher dimensions. The process usually involves being activated by a trained practitioner during a deep meditative state.

Downloading is a term used to describe the New Age phenomenon of sudden, large amounts of information literally downloading into an individual's mind. Consisting of information that is generally metaphysical.

Earthkeepers are spiritual stewards devoted to the well-being of Gaia. Earthkeepers are souls who carry a sacred responsibility to nurture, protect, and collaborate with the living intelligence of the planet. Whether through environmental activism, indigenous wisdom, permaculture, energy healing, or intuitive communion with nature, Earthkeepers serve as bridge-beings between the ancient memory of the Earth and the evolutionary future of humanity. In the framework of CP, they embody the frequency of reciprocal nourishment—giving to the Earth as they receive from her, and walking the path of becoming with rooted reverence. While Starseeds often look to the stars, Earthkeepers listen deeply to the soil, waters, and pulse of life beneath their feet, offering an essential counterbalance and grounding to the cosmic call.

Egregore is a collective energetic entity or thought form generated by a group's shared focus, emotions, and beliefs. It can be benevolent or destructive, depending on the frequency of its creators. Often described as a "meme with momentum," egregores form in the etheric realms and can subtly influence individuals within their field. In CP, egregores are understood as amplifiers of collective consciousness. They mirror both our highest ideals and our most profound distortions. From healing lineages to fear-based cults, every group builds an egregore, whether they are conscious of it or not. The egregore becomes real when enough people feed it, and it becomes even more powerful when enough people forget they created it.

Energy Field refers to the subtle, multidimensional matrix of light, frequency, and information that surrounds and infuses the human body. It serves as the vibrational interface between the physical, emotional, mental, and spiritual aspects of being. The term is often synonymous with the Luminous Energy Field (LEF) and the Human Energy System (HES). Our awareness of this field expands as we evolve, revealing new structures and capacities within the body of light. It is both a mirror of consciousness and a vehicle of becoming.

Energy Grid is a web of lines or axiatonal lines of electromagnetic energy that connects all matter to all matter throughout the universe.

Energy Medicine (EM) is the term that became known in the early 1980s for the branch of alternative or complementary medicine that utilizes subtle, putative energies or light to heal. Healing with subtle energies is documented throughout history and in all indigenous cultures. The Chinese acupuncture system is based on directing the flow of subtle or vital energy, which they refer to as Chi or Qi (pronounced "chee"). Jesus Christ remains the world's most renowned healer. Although not typically considered an energy medicine practitioner, it is generally understood that he utilized light to heal. Energy medicine is becoming increasingly mainstream and encompasses a wide variety of modalities, including acupuncture,

Glossary

acupressure, chakra balancing, Reiki (offered in many mainstream hospitals), The Reconnection, Pranic Healing, Emotional Freedom Technique (EFT), Shamanism, or any combination thereof. EM is a branch of Alternative or Complementary Medicine that includes various modalities. EM got its official name in the late 1980s when the International Society for the Study of Subtle Energies and Energy Medicine (ISSSEEM) was founded in Boulder, Colorado.

Energy Psychology (EP) is a mind-body healing approach that combines traditional psychology principles with energy-based techniques. It was formally named and developed by Fred Gallo, Ph.D., and has been significantly advanced by the work of the Association for Comprehensive Energy Psychology (ACEP). EP operates on the premise that unresolved emotional trauma and limiting beliefs are not only stored in the mind and body but also within the body's energy systems, such as meridians, chakras, and biofields. By stimulating specific acupressure points while focusing on emotional issues, clients can experience rapid shifts in thought patterns, emotional states, and even physiological symptoms. Modalities within EP include Thought Field Therapy (TFT), Emotional Freedom Techniques (EFT), Tapas Acupressure Technique (TAT), and other integrative tools that restore balance to the body's energetic and psychological systems. EP is increasingly recognized for its effectiveness in treating anxiety, trauma, PTSD, phobias, and other psychosomatic conditions.

Entrainment refers to the natural phenomenon in which two or more rhythmic systems begin synchronizing. In physics and biology, this can be observed when pendulums swing in unison or heartbeats align. In energy medicine and consciousness evolution, entrainment refers to the process by which individuals, groups, or planetary fields synchronize their frequencies, whether through shared intention, presence, breath, or resonance. Entrainment is not about conformity, but rather coherence; it is about how nervous systems regulate together, how brainwaves attune in meditation, and how higher vibrational states can gently elevate those around them. In CP, entrainment is understood as both a healing mechanism and a sacred reminder: we are wired to influence and be influenced, and with awareness, we can become entraining agents of coherence, love, and light.

Epigenetics is a branch of science that studies changes and the functioning of the genome that are in addition to or above the DNA sequence, or are not derived from changes to the DNA sequence. In contrast, genetics is concerned only with heredity and variations in gene patterns.

Esoteric is the term that points to the "internal" world. It is associated with spirituality, metaphysics, and the occult, i.e., all things considered hidden or secret.

Kaleidoscope for Becoming: A Grimoire of Revolution

Essential Self is the essence of the human being, which is spiritual or divine. It is the opposite of the egoic self.

Ethereal is often associated with things that are airy, otherworldly, or beyond material reality. It is sometimes used to describe a layer or dimension of the mind or consciousness.

Exoteric is a term that points to the "external" world. It would thus be associated with religious teachings that deal with dogma and external rules.

Extremism is a rigid and uncompromising adherence to a set of beliefs, values, or ideologies, often accompanied by the rejection or demonization of differing perspectives. Extremism can manifest in various contexts, including political, religious, spiritual, or social spheres, and is often fueled by fear, anger, perceived injustice, or a desire for certainty in uncertain times. From an evolutionary psychological perspective, extremism is seen as a psychological and spiritual imbalance rooted in fragmentation and disconnection from wholeness. It reflects the ego's attempt to impose order through absolutism, denying the complexity and nuance inherent in evolutionary growth. Developing our capacity for true awakening requires the ability to hold paradoxes, remain open to diverse viewpoints, and cultivate compassion even for those with whom we disagree. Extremism dissolves when coherence, humility, and a willingness to engage in dialogue are restored. These are all basic tenets of CP.

Evolucentia *(eh-voh-loo-SEN-sha)* (n.) is a neologism blending evolution and lucent (light-bearing). Evolucentia is the radiant current of becoming that arises from the Ground of All Being. It is the luminous expression of consciousness unfolding through energy, frequency, and vibration. It serves as an evolutionary tide sourced from the Zero Point, where all potential exists in the perfect stillness of infinite possibilities. Evolucentia describes the soul's impulse to become light-aware, to evolve biologically, intellectually, and vibrationally. It's the shimmering thread of intelligent light moving through the Human Energy System, awakening the Homo luminous blueprint —a quantum invitation to embody the light of one's becoming, sourced from the silent core of creation itself. It updates the CP formula for $\uparrow$ QOL $\propto$ $\uparrow$ QOLEI $\times$ Coherence of Energy, Frequency, and Vibration.

Evolution has come to mean more than the biological paradigm of Darwinism. In today's evolving paradigm, the evolutionary process includes the development of consciousness. This concept is becoming understood as the ultimate component of our survival as a species.

Evolutionary is an individual who accepts that evolution is a spiritual process, understands that the transformation of our world depends on our willingness to deliberately and consciously evolve ourselves, recognizes that the survival of our species and our planet depends on evolution, and is committed to the evolutionary process. **Stay tuned for a wave of vibrant new descriptors,**

such as Evolutionista and Evolutionaro, *evolving* into the collective lexicon as these concepts catch on.

Evolutionary Eyes develop once we accept the newly evolving esoteric paradigm mentioned above. Everything we observe becomes a function of the process. All disasters, both man-made and natural, as well as all struggles, aches, and pains, begin to make sense as we understand that negativity comes to the surface for its purification and natural order.

Evolutionary Impulse is a term used by Evolutionaries and futurists to describe the spark of creation, which occurs when something is created out of nothing, initiating the forward movement of the evolutionary trajectory.

Evolutionary Kaleidoscope is presented here as a central metaphor—an invitation to visualize the infinite, continuously unfolding, ever-changing, and multidimensionally radiant expressions of creation. Just as a kaleidoscope offers shifting patterns of color and form with every subtle turn, so does consciousness's evolution reveal itself in fractals of insight, transformation, and possibility. Rather than a linear or fixed process, evolution is seen through this lens as a spiraling dance of becoming—alive, dynamic, and constantly reorganizing itself in response to vibration, intention, and awareness. Each turn of the kaleidoscope reflects a new level of perception, a fresh perspective, and a configuration of inner and outer reality. In *A Kaleidoscope for Becoming*, this metaphor serves as a visual aid and a spiritual principle. It honors the beauty of impermanence, the creativity of chaos, and the sacredness of nonlinear growth. The Evolutionary Kaleidoscope reminds us that change is not something to fear—it is the very artistry of the cosmos in motion. Through the lens of CP, each person is invited to become both observer and creator—witnessing past patterns, reframing the present, and turning the kaleidoscope of their soul toward ever-brighter expressions of truth, love, and light.

Evolutionary Psychology is a branch of science that consists of the study of human adaptations. It encompasses the neurobiological functions of the nervous system, as well as the brain's functions in language, memory, perception, and behavior.

Evolutionary Spirituality is both a global social movement in its early stages and a concept that posits the innate impulse to evolve is as much a spiritual impulse as a biological one. It is best known for its association with Sri Aurobindo (1872–1950), one of India's most prominent leaders, who first gained prominence politically and later developed a spiritual following. He is regarded as an Evolutionary and is world-renowned for his teachings. His basic tenet is that man is to transcend himself (become divine), and once we develop our higher mind, we will have a "luminous thought-mind" with elevated powers and mental sight. He described the crown chakra as being open and functioning correctly. Pir Vilayat Inayat Khan (1916-2004) was

Kaleidoscope for Becoming: A Grimoire of Revolution

perhaps the greatest Sufi teacher of this century. He taught that the universe is evolving as we become more participatory in its manifestation through observation and awakening to the process.

Evolutionary Trajectory is a term used by Evolutionaries and futurists to account for all forward movement in the universe. The forward-moving thrust provides individuals with a sense of direction for a positive future (no matter the appearance of the present).

Evolutionary Worldview did not exist before the 1930s. Over the last eighty years, there has been an exponential growth in awareness that consciousness and evolution are nearly synonymous. As humanity develops its evolutionary perspective, the evolutionary worldview evolves in the collective unconscious, also known as the Noosphere.

Fear-based Consciousness refers to a state of awareness dominated by survival instincts, scarcity thinking, control dynamics, and disconnection from the heart or higher self. It is often rooted in unresolved trauma or conditioning and manifests through anxiety, aggression, judgment, and resistance to change. In spiritual evolution, this is the density we are learning to transmute—individually and collectively—as we transition from 3D to 5D, moving toward unity, coherence, and love-based awareness. CP presents it as the Egoic or monkey mind, drawing on New Age and Buddhist teachings.

4chan[19] is an anonymous online imageboard, originally launched in 2003, that evolved into a chaotic breeding ground for internet memes, trolling, and radical discourse. 4chan is the birthplace of both the Anonymous collective and the early cryptic messages of the QAnon conspiracy movement. Known for its lack of moderation and its cloak of anonymity, 4chan has fostered both viral creativity and dangerous disinformation. From a CP perspective, 4chan represents the shadowy undercurrent of the digital collective, ever reminding us to engage with the evolutionary survival skills of discernment, coherence, and alignment with universal truth.

Frequency is the rate at which energy vibrates. In CP, frequency is the *refinement* of vibration, the tonal quality of your energy field as it oscillates through time and space. Higher frequencies resonate with clarity, love, coherence, and expanded awareness, while lower frequencies reflect density, distortion, or fragmentation. Frequency is not a matter of judgment; it is an indicator of resonance. It reveals the level of consciousness you are currently attuned to and the experiences you magnetize.

Futurist(s) are scholars, scientists, innovators, or any individuals concerned with the future, specifically the survival of humankind. However, they study

---

[19] Rather than strict adherence to traditional alphabetization or definitions, this entry has been placed here deliberately being offered as living transmission intended to spark insight, remembrance, and resonance within readers.

historical and current trends to indicate what is coming, not necessarily to predict specifics.

Greys are among the most reported extraterrestrial species, often described as small, thin beings with large heads, gray skin, and black almond-shaped eyes. Associated with UFO sightings and abduction narratives, they are said to originate from the Zeta Reticuli star system. Interpretations range from technologically advanced observers to beings seeking to reconnect with lost emotional or spiritual capacities.

Grimoire (pronounced *grim-wahr*) is traditionally known as a book of magical knowledge—a sacred compilation of spells, invocations, symbols, and esoteric wisdom. But in a more modern or metaphysical sense, a grimoire can be any personal or collective record of mystical insight, soul technologies, or sacred teachings.

Holographic Initiations are transformative experiences that operate simultaneously across multiple layers of time, space, and consciousness. Unlike linear growth, where progress unfolds step by step, a holographic initiation is encoded with multidimensional meaning, simultaneously activating healing, awakening, and remembrance on several levels. These initiations often appear as symbolic or catalytic life events: an illness, a spiritual awakening, a relationship rupture, a synchronicity so precise it feels otherworldly. What makes them "holographic" is that they do not just impact the present moment—they ripple through past timelines, ancestral lines, parallel lives, and future potentials, reorganizing the soul's blueprint toward greater coherence. In CP, holographic initiations are sacred invitations from the soul to evolve exponentially. They are not punishments or random occurrences but *intelligent orchestrations* designed to compress time, reveal inner truth, and open portals to higher-dimensional awareness. Each initiation or experience is a spiral within the spiral—a fractal moment of becoming that echoes through the kaleidoscope of your multidimensional self.

Holy Work is the term used in CP for quantum consciousness-enhancement activities. *Holy Work* includes talk therapy, any form of meditation, prayer, ritual, ceremony, physical activity, energy medicine, and energetic-body work designed to reach higher levels of awareness and permanently improve QOL.

Homo luminous is a term with roots in ancient indigenous cultures, introduced to holistic circles and popularized by Alberto Villoldo, Ph.D. Evolutionaries believe that Homo sapiens are developing into Homo-luminous light beings.

Homo universalis is a term used to describe the species Homo sapiens, which may evolve to recognize itself as one with each other and with the universe. This term also indicates the species has evolved into an intergalactic cooperative existence.

Human Energy System (HES) is the anatomy of all the structures that sustain the life force, Chi, Ki, or Prana. The HES varies within differing traditions.

However, most concur that seven layers of energy surround the body—in the aura and seven spinning discs of energy, called the chakras. There are also hundreds of minor chakras at the physical body's joints and meridian points, as well as energetic cords and bundles of cords, each with their highly specialized functions. Science is beginning to verify its existence, and as more people awaken to the HES through yoga, meditation, and other deliberately activating and strengthening practices, the entire system is revealing itself as an ever-evolving and unfolding complex creation. For example, as the collective recognizes the eighth chakra, it further activates within the collective HES, as well as for the individuals working with it.

Hybrids are typically understood as beings who consist of a blend of human and non-human DNA, either through direct genetic interweaving (in utero or through galactic seeding) or energetic merging. They may have physical, psychological, or energetic traits that reflect this blending. Some hybrids are said to be part of intentional multi-dimensional programs to assist Earth's evolution.

Imaginal Cells are the cells of change in a biologically evolving organism. A prime example is the metamorphosis of the butterfly. The imaginal cells exist in the caterpillar and hold the *image* of the butterfly. The caterpillar's immune system perceives the foreign matter as a threat and responds by attacking it. Eventually, however, the imaginal cells outnumber the old caterpillar cells, and the butterfly develops unencumbered. Evolutionaries, including Lightworkers, Starseeds, and Earthkeepers, are considered the imaginal cells of the New Humanity[20].

Infodemic is a modern term describing the overwhelming flood of accurate and false information that makes it difficult for individuals to discern truth from distortion. Coined by the World Health Organization, the term "infodemic" originally referred to the information crisis during the COVID-19 pandemic, but its relevance extends to all eras of rapid information dissemination. From a psychological perspective, it can represent a form of information trauma, where the nervous system and psyche become overloaded by conflicting messages, conspiracy theories, and fear-based narratives. This state can lead to confusion, anxiety, poor judgment, or withdrawal. CP practices that cultivate inner coherence, discernment, and anchoring into trusted guidance rooted in love, truth, and integrity are the antidote, as well as limiting exposure to chaotic sources.

Integrative Medicine (IM) blends the Western medical model with alternative or complementary treatments.

---

[20] It is no coincidence that as the 2012 phenomenon awakened vast numbers of 'imaginal cells' the Dark Enlightenment movement and other conspiritual narratives rose in tandem, complicating the spiritual landscape and making discernment more critical than ever.

Glossary

Interspiritual refers to the emerging practice of discerning and honoring shared truths across the world's religious and spiritual traditions. The term gained recognition through the work of Brother Wayne Teasdale. He envisioned Interspirituality as a practical, global spirituality that transcends doctrine to unite humanity in the service of healing, justice, and planetary sustainability. Rather than erasing differences, Interspirituality invites a deeper listening across traditions to uncover universal wisdom and collaborative action. While often confused with Interfaith, the two are distinct: Interfaith centers on dialogue between different religious institutions, emphasizing tolerance and cooperation while maintaining theological boundaries. Interspirituality, by contrast, is experiential, contemplative, and integrative. It invites the seeker to engage directly with the mystical and ethical essence of multiple traditions. The goal is to deepen inner transformation and foster universal compassion, rather than blending beliefs. In CP, Interspirituality is recognized as a path to spiritual coherence. It is an embodied awareness that the truth of Oneness may speak in many languages, yet still resonate with a single Divine frequency.

Jinn are supernatural beings in Arabic mythology, also known as genies in many cultures. They are believed to be spirits of a lower nature than heavenly angels and can assume human or animal form. Therefore, they are often associated with possession or mental illness. The Arabic meaning of the word Jinn is "something that is concealed from sight," so they share traits with both angels and humans, such as free will; they can be easily summoned to do the bidding of the sorcerer or summoner.

Kālī is the fierce goddess of time, transformation, destruction, and liberation in Hindu tradition. Often depicted with dark skin, a garland of skulls, and a wild, untamed presence, Kālī represents the unstoppable force of change and the dissolution of illusion. She destroys egoic attachments, falsehoods, and stagnant patterns, making way for rebirth, awakening, and sovereignty.

Light Body, Luminous Energy Field (LEF) See Human Energy System (HES).

Light Language is a multidimensional mode of communication that bypasses the logical mind and transmits frequencies of healing, remembrance, and activation directly to the soul and energy body. Often expressed through spontaneous vocalizations, written symbols, hand movements, or inner visual streams, Light Language is not decoded through traditional linguistics but felt through resonance. It functions as a vibrational carrier of Light, Energy, and Information (QOLEI), awakening latent capacities within the DNA and reconnecting us to galactic lineages, cosmic memory, and future modalities of nonverbal, supraconscious expression. Within the framework of CP, Light Language is considered a sacred technology of becoming—evidence of our evolution beyond linear communication toward the radiant embodiment of Homo luminous, the precursor to Homo universalis.

Loosh is typically considered the subtle energy harvested from the suffering and negative emotions (and often purposefully instigated) by higher-dimensional entities for their sustenance. This understanding aligns with Gnostic ideas that archons utilize the Earth as an energy source for humans, whom they control and manipulate. However, the term has recently expanded to include positive emotions such as love and joy.

Lulz is a slang derivative of "laugh out loud" (LOL) and refers to the amusement or entertainment gained at someone else's expense through pranks, trolling, or the disruption of social norms. In the online communities of 4chan and early Anonymous, actions were frequently justified as being "for the lulz," meaning done purely for the twisted pleasure of causing confusion, outrage, or absurdity. Unlike simple humor, lulz often carries an undercurrent of mockery, nihilism, or even cruelty, where the suffering or dismay of others is the punchline. It reflects the darker side of internet anonymity, where moral accountability is stripped away, and chaos is prized over compassion. From a CP perspective, *lulz lulls us back into degenerative sleep* (described by philosophers such as Manly P. Hall), a state of unconsciousness where the sacred responsibility of discernment is abandoned. In this way, lulz has become not just a joke, but a tool to induce spiritual regression in the digital age.

Meliorism is a philosophical and metaphysical perspective that affirms that the world and society naturally improve, and this improvement is enhanced and accelerated by human effort. Meliorism aligns with the evolutionary worldview and underlies the democratic philosophical position of liberalism.

Meridian Points are electromagnetic palpable spots located along the body's meridian lines. They are treated with needles (acupuncture), pressure (acupressure), or Emotional Freedom Technique (EFT) (Meridian tapping) sessions to release blocked energy and heal the body of disease. New research indicates they are not only energy pathways but also pathways of light and information.

Merkabah is a vehicle that can be created or accessed (depending on various teachings) through visualization, raising consciousness and vibratory rates, and traveling to different dimensions.

Metaphysics is the philosophical concern or branch of science that studies the fundamental nature of all reality, the seen and unseen, the visible and the invisible. It is the study of—and the subsequent description of—being and knowing. It is concerned with whatever the fundamental nature is that anything must have to exist.

Metaphysician or (Metaphysicist) can be a student of metaphysics. However, it is best to declare oneself a metaphysician only with proper certification.

Several esoteric and mystery schools provide in-depth studies and certifications for that purpose.

Multidimensional Self refers to the totality of your being across space, time, frequency, and form. It is the soul's expression, not limited to one life, body, or timeline, but exists simultaneously across many realms and realities. This Self encompasses the Higher Self, Galactic Self, Shadow Self, Inner Child, Future Self, and Ascended Self—all facets of the same being, each reflecting a distinct aspect of our journey through creation. As we awaken, we consciously access these layers, retrieving soul fragments, healing karmic patterns, and integrating forgotten gifts. In CP, honoring the Multidimensional Self is central to becoming a Supraconscious Creator who recognizes that healing, manifestation, and ascension are not linear processes but holographic initiations. We are not just evolving; we remember ourselves as galaxies in motion.

Mysticism is the practice or experience of altered states of reality or consciousness, typically associated with divine union and spiritual revelation for transformation. There are numerous religions and a variety of classified types of mysticism.

Mystical Experience is a spiritual revelation, vision, or state of consciousness achieved through the practice of mysticism in various forms, including meditation, prayer, ecstatic or trance dance, and intuition. Many of these experiences often end when the practice has ended or shortly after that.

New Age is a social movement that typically begins about three decades before the turn of any century. It is a time of natural introspection when humans evaluate the past and anticipate the new. Our current New Age movement began in the 1970s, and as the term gained popularity, it became associated with the Peace Movement. The term and many associated practices have continued to gain traction in the mainstream over the last few decades. It is now understood to be the utilization of eclectic combinations of age-old wisdom from various religious, philosophical, metaphysical, and occult teachings, blended with contemporary scientific, medical, and psychological practices and insights from transpersonal psychology, with the overarching purpose of improving both the individual and the collective.

New Human. See **The New Human**

New Humanity. See **The New Humanity**

New Thought is a predominantly religious, philosophically, and spiritually oriented movement that began in the late 1800s. The New Thought movement gave rise to three major religious denominations that remain active today: Science of Mind, Unity Church, and The Church of Divine Science.

Nihilism is a philosophical worldview rooted in the belief that life has no inherent meaning, purpose, or value. Often arising in response to disillusionment or existential despair, nihilism can lead to apathy, detachment, or a rejection of moral and spiritual frameworks. In contrast, *A Kaleidoscope for Becoming* offers a melioristic and evolutionary perspective that sees meaning as something we co-create through consciousness, connection, and soul alignment.

Noosphere comes from the Greek *nous* (mind) and *sphaira* (sphere), which is considered by most to be an emergent sheath of collective human thought, the third great layer or "sphere" of Earth's unfolding. Just as the biosphere (the second layer, teeming with biological life) evolved from the geosphere (the first layer of inanimate matter), the Noosphere arises from the biosphere through the forces of thinking, reflection, culture, technology, and spiritual awakening. Initially introduced by Russian geochemist Vladimir Vernadsky, the concept gained evolutionary momentum through Teilhard de Chardin's Law of Complexity and Consciousness, which posits that as systems grow in complexity, they also deepen in consciousness. The Noosphere is not simply a mental field—it is the psychic atmosphere of Earth, infused with intention, encoded with wisdom, and increasingly shaped by our co-creative participation. Thinkers such as Barbara Marx Hubbard and José Argüelles have expanded the implications of the Noosphere for planetary evolution. Today, the rapid rise of artificial intelligence—as a mirror of our collective cognition—amplifies this global *mindfield*[21] in real time. In the vision of *Celestial Psychology*®, the Noosphere is where supraconscious evolution begins: a life-enhancing expression of humanity's soul, maturing toward coherence, compassion, and luminous purpose.

Overself is the spiritual self, soul, higher self, or divine self.

Past Life Regression is the practice of utilizing hypnosis to access memories of one's past lives.

Photobiomodulation (PBM) is a non-invasive therapeutic technique that uses specific wavelengths of light—typically red or near-infrared—to stimulate cellular function, enhance tissue repair, and reduce inflammation. PBM primarily works by delivering light to the mitochondria, the cell's energy centers, where it enhances ATP production and supports metabolic efficiency. Unlike heat-based therapies, PBM does not rely on thermal effects. Instead, it promotes biological restoration by encouraging coherence within and between cells. Clinical studies have shown promising results in pain relief, wound healing, skin rejuvenation, and neurological support.

Prana is a Sanskrit term meaning "life force." Because the Sanskrit root *pra* is "to fill" and the Latin root is complete, one can say that Pranic energy is full of vital life. Pranic Healing® is based on cleansing and energizing the chakras (major energy centers). This modality is promising for relieving symptoms,

---

21 Mindfield is a poetic neologism blending "mind" and "field," used here to evoke the subtle terrain of collective consciousness. It also plays on the word "minefield," hinting at both the power and complexity inherent in navigating the evolving Noosphere.

Glossary

balancing the chakras, and cleansing the aura (energy body). It is a no-touch modality.

Pronoia is the opposite of paranoia; it is the empowering perception that the universe is conspiring in our favor and that life is unfolding with benevolence, synchronicity, and unseen support. Coined by Grateful Dead lyricist John Perry Barlow and later popularized by visionary thinker Rob Brezsny, pronoia reflects a worldview rooted in trust, abundance, and cosmic collaboration. In the context of CP, pronoia is not naïve optimism—it is an attunement to the vibrational truth that we are co-creators in a benevolent, evolving cosmos. It invites us to notice the subtle winks of grace, signs, and serendipities that remind us we are not alone and were made for the magic of BE-coming.

QAnon is a conspiracy movement that began on the anonymous imageboard 4chan in 2017, when a poster using the name "Q" claimed to have high-level government clearance and insider knowledge of a hidden battle between good and evil within governments and global institutions. QAnon combined spiritual language, patriotism, anti-establishment rhetoric, and recycled conspiracy tropes, attracting a vast and diverse online following. From a CP perspective, QAnon illustrates the dangers of unexamined narratives that blend legitimate skepticism with misinformation, projection, and mythologized fantasy. It serves as a modern reminder that true awakening does not come from external authorities, cryptic messages, or digital prophets, but from inner discernment, coherence, and alignment with universal truth. We are reminded that discernment is not only a spiritual practice but also a survival skill.

Qualia is Latin for 'raw feel' or the essence or quality of something that can only be known by direct experience. Typically, qualia refers to the nature of a mental state, such as anger or pain, rather than an object or experience. Specifically, qualia refers to the 'what it is like' phenomenon, or the experience itself.

Quality-of-Life (QOL) is a phrase typically used to describe the overall quality of an individual's existence. The psychological quality or one's state of mind influences all other aspects of life, such as health, finances, and relationships.

Quantity-of-Light-Energy-Information (QOLEI) is a formula created for CP to articulate what occurs during the Holy Work of consciousness-raising and quantum consciousness-enhancements.

Quality-and-Quantity-of Coherence in Energy, Frequency, and Vibration (QQ-CEFV) This term refines the understanding of coherence as a multidimensional force, emphasizing not only how well (quality) but also how strongly and consistently (quantity) coherence is embodied within the subtle energy system, and is integrated into the upgraded formula below QQ-CEFV.

QOL Formula: $\wedge$ **QOL** α $\wedge$ **QOLEI x QQ-CEFV**. Initially introduced in 2013, this foundational equation states that an increase in Quality of Life

(QOL) occurs in direct proportion to an increase in the Quantity of Light, Energy, and Information (QOLEI) brought in through consciousness-raising and quantum-enhancement practices. This elementary articulation laid the groundwork for further development and refinement of its vibrational expression. In its 2025 evolved form, the formula now includes an essential multiplier: $\wedge$ **QOL** α $\wedge$ **QOLEI x QQ-CEFV**, where QQ-CEFV represents the quality and quantity of energy, frequency, and vibration coherence. Together, these principles form the basis of the Evolucentia Model, a living framework for understanding how subtle forces shape the radiant architecture of well-being and becoming.

Quantum (quanta - plural) is the most fundamental or the smallest unit or quantity of energy, light, or photon. A quantum acts both like a particle and like an energy wave.

Quantum Physics studies the behavior of quanta, specifically matter and energy, at the molecular level. Max Planck is attributed with its inception.

Quantum Theory is one of the most significant discoveries in physics this century, as it describes the nature of the universe through subatomic particles. Quantum Theory radically differs from anything prior, especially relativity, which explains the nature of the universe through its most significant elements—space and time.

Quantum Worldview is a contemporary phrase that appears to have been coined by Amit Goswami, Ph.D. He postulates that the Quantum Worldview will open the door to a scientific understanding of all our experiences, thereby elevating consciousness to align with the forward trajectory of evolution.

Rabbit Holes are a metaphor for deep, often disorienting journeys into complex or fringe ideas, usually through endless exploration of theories with online information, especially videos and social media. In CP, "falling down rabbit holes" symbolizes the soul's urge to seek hidden truths and more profound meaning. Yet, it warns of becoming lost in illusion, misinformation, or obsessive thinking. The evolutionary challenge is to explore complex and fringe ideas with discernment, to remain grounded in coherence, and to distinguish between fascination and emotional or visceral reactions and fact. True wisdom lies not in how far we descend into the rabbit hole, or how deeply we 'feel' something, but in how well we return from the exploration with clarity and integration.

Reciprocal Nourishment is a sacred exchange of energy between dimensions. Reciprocal nourishment is the mutually beneficial flow (movement) of light, love, and frequency between human beings and benevolent higher intelligence, such as Ascended Masters, spirit allies, and the healing field of Source itself. Unlike extractive or parasitic models of energy (as found in lower-dimensional interpretations of *loosh*), this dynamic is rooted in reverence, joy, and co-creation. When a practitioner of *13th Octave LaHoChi* or any high-vibrational modality enters a state of coherence, awe, and willing devotion, they emit a vibrational signature that enhances their healing potential and uplifts and empowers the beings they are assisting. This energetic offering often manifests as goosebumps of gratitude, tears of joy and remembrance, and songs of devotion, becoming a form of spiritual sustenance that nourishes the web of light. Reciprocal nourishment reminds us that we are not merely invoking help but engaging in a living and loving relationship. The more consciously and coherently we give, the more radiance we receive.

Reincarnation is an accepted concept in many of the world's religions, including those within the Spiritism and New Age circles. The basic teaching is that the soul of a deceased person or animal returns to another physical life in accordance with or in proportion to the lessons the soul did or did not learn from the previous lifetime.

Relative healing refers to observable changes to the physical, emotional, energetic, and mental bodies. (See Ultimate healing.)

Resonance is a state of vibrational harmony between two or more systems. In metaphysics and CP, resonance occurs when frequencies align, amplify, or entrain, creating a field of coherence that transcends separation. Resonance is how healing happens, truth is felt, and connection is recognized beyond logic. To be "in resonance" with a person, idea, or energy is to experience soul-level attunement, a felt sense of alignment that vibrates with meaning. Resonance is the subtle intelligence that guides synchronicity, intuitive knowing, and quantum entanglement in the living universe. Resonance is not limited to living beings. The frequencies of inanimate objects can also entrain, as in the phenomenon of fork-bending. When a bent fork is placed next to an unbent one and held in focused visualization, the molecular structure of the unbent fork can begin to entrain to the energetic imprint of the bent one, revealing that intention, coherence, and focus can alter form at the subatomic level.

Reptilians, reptilian humanoids, reptiloids, or draconians are a purported race of extraterrestrial beings whose presence, whether understood as literal beings or archetypal symbols of fear-based control, invites us to deepen our discernment, integrate the shadow aspects of consciousness, and reclaim our Divine Sovereignty.

Sacred Geometry is a modern umbrella term encompassing the mystical, spiritual, and philosophical framework that sees geometric forms, patterns, and proportions as blueprints of divine intelligence. From the Flower of Life, the Golden Ratio, Metatron's Cube, and the Fibonacci Spiral to the spiral of galaxies and the structure of DNA, sacred geometry reveals itself as the underlying architecture of creation, the true language of the cosmos. These patterns are symbols and vibrational maps of consciousness rooted in ancient traditions, from Egyptian temples to Platonic solids.

Schumann Resonance is a set of extremely low-frequency (ELF) electromagnetic waves that reverberate between the Earth's surface and the ionosphere, an atmospheric cavity that acts like a planetary drum. Discovered in the 1950s by physicist Winfried Otto Schumann, its fundamental frequency hums around 7.83 Hz, often referred to as the "heartbeat of the Earth." Scientifically, this resonance is generated by global lightning activity and provides a measurable rhythm to the planet's energetic environment. Metaphysically, it is believed to mirror the Alpha brainwave state, fostering a relaxed, meditative awareness and serving as a subtle tuning fork for human consciousness. CP considers it part of the Earth's vibrational scaffolding, a background frequency that supports coherence, grounding, and evolutionary attunement. As Earth and humanity evolve together, fluctuations in this resonance are seen as natural and invitations to harmonize with deeper layers of planetary and cosmic intelligence.

Self-Evolution is a concept introduced by Carl Jung, which posits the continuing incarnation of the individual's transcendental or higher Self through the integration of the personality. Evolutionaries promote this concept, such as Barbara Marx Hubbard, who wrote on her website, "Self-evolution, then, is the process of becoming a co-creator with the impulse of creation itself. The maturation of our species finds its expression in each of us unfolding the divine within." This Self is seen as the essential aspect of our being, directly animated by Source, by Spirit. It is the localized, individualized aspect of the Process of Creation, the God force, and the Impulse of Evolution. This Self has often been projected onto Gods and ascended beings. Now, as the human species slowly matures, this Self is incarnating as our own essence, our own incarnation of spirit, our own individual expression of the divine.

Shape Shifters are mythological, interdimensional, or energetic beings who can change form at will. Found in indigenous traditions, folklore, and esoteric literature across cultures, shapeshifters may appear as animals, humans, spirits, or hybrids. They often symbolize adaptability, hidden identities, or transformational power. In metaphysical teachings, shape-shifters can also refer to benevolent or deceptive entities who present themselves in shifting guises across dimensions or energetic frequencies. They may be guides, guardians, or tricksters, challenging our ability to perceive truth beyond appearances. Psychologically, the shape-shifter archetype represents aspects of the self that are fluid, elusive, or in a state of flux. Those parts of us that resist categorization mask our true nature or move between personas as a survival mechanism. In the Holy Work of consciousness-raising, recognizing the shape-shifter within can be a decisive step toward integration and wholeness.

Shadow Work is the process of consciously exploring the unconscious—the parts of the self that have been repressed, denied, or disowned due to fear, trauma, cultural conditioning, or ego defense. These hidden aspects, known collectively as the shadow, often carry emotional charge, ancestral pain, unmet needs, and, paradoxically, untapped wisdom and power. First named by Carl Jung, the shadow is not inherently "bad;" rather, it represents what has been cast out of the light of awareness. Shadow Work invites us to retrieve and integrate these lost parts, transforming shame into compassion, projection into ownership, and fragmentation into wholeness. Shadow Work is not separate from awakening but an *initiation* into it. The light path inevitably leads through the valley of our unhealed darkness. The shadow's integration gives spiritual growth depth, stability, and authenticity.

Spiritual Bypassing is a term coined by psychologist John Welwood to describe the tendency to use spiritual beliefs or practices to avoid facing unresolved emotional wounds, personal responsibility, or psychological pain. In CP, spiritual bypassing is seen as an ego defense that masks true healing behind positivity, detachment, or transcendent ideals. True awakening requires the willingness to fully feel, process, and integrate all aspects of human experience—not escape from them.

Starseeds are souls whose *origin* lies outside of Earth, often from other star systems (like Sirius, Pleiades, Arcturus, etc.), higher dimensions, or non-physical realms. They incarnate into human bodies through traditional birth but often feel a deep soul remembrance of having come from "elsewhere." Their "otherworldliness" is more *energetic and soul-based* than physical.

Subtle Energy is the vital/divine/spiritual force or life force found in all things in the entire universe.

Supraconscious Creators is the name designated in CP for the next genus of humanity, of which the new species of Homo luminous, Homo angelicus, Homo universalis, and others will most likely be included.

Tachyons are sub-atomic particles that have mass yet travel faster than the speed of light. They can only exist in other higher-dimensional realms outside our 3-D Cartesian, Newtonian understanding of the universe. Operating outside of linear time and ordinary spacetime constraints, tachyons challenge the very fabric of classical physics. Science fiction popularized them as a means of time travel. According to Vedic scripture, the word for "speed of the mind" is Manojava. It is also poetically translated as "divine wind" or "essence of the gods." Manojava is often associated with the deity Hanuman, who symbolizes swiftness and agility. It is easy to see how this concept inspired the idea that tachyons are "the stuff the Gods are made of," particles of divine intelligence capable of bridging matter, mind, and spirit.

Temporal Connection is a telepathic, soul-level link that transcends linear time. It bridges human consciousness with nonhuman intelligence, such as divine beings, extraterrestrials, or interdimensional guides. These connections arise through vibrational resonance, not physical proximity, and often emerge during states of heightened coherence, such as deep meditation or energy healing. While related to channeling and mediumship, a temporal connection emphasizes the frequency-based alignment that facilitates such communication, particularly with beings whose awareness spans across dimensions and timelines.

The Great Shift or **The Shift** are terms that have gained momentum over the last decade to designate this time in history as a period in which the consciousness (both individual and collective) of the human species shifts from being self-centered or ego-centric to energy- or divine-centered and universally oriented. There is a tremendous consensus among the scientific, astronomical, historical, philosophical, theosophical, archaeological, and indigenous communities, as well as visionaries and prophets, that this is a literal occurrence. The term became nearly synonymous with the end of the world, which was predicted by doomsayers to occur on December 21, 2012. This date marked the end of the last recorded (5200-year cycle) ancient Mayan calendar. Contemporary Mayan elders insisted that this did not mean the end of the world, but rather the end of a world that they knew, signifying a new beginning. (See definition of The New Humanity) Specifically, to differing cultural factions, The Shift indicates the following: the Second Coming of Christ or the Christification of the Planet; the return of the Mayan god, Quetzalcoatl, the plumed serpent; the collapse of the third dimension into the fourth and fifth dimensions where humans will dwell as gods; humanity's (only the righteous or the ready) Ascension into heaven; living in abundance and Oneness with the Cosmos; deliverance into Utopia with help from friendly intergalactic races; and the disappearance of the modern-day Neanderthal man. Some researchers and spiritual historians have noted an eerie and fascinating astrological and astronomical resemblance between our current age and the era when Neanderthals became extinct. Just as that shift marked the rise of Homo sapiens, today's Shift may mark the emergence of *Homo luminous*—a being of expanded awareness, energetic mastery, and heart coherence. Generally, The Shift is considered a shift in human consciousness, a historical landmark of evolution when Homo sapiens wake up and realize that cooperation, along with the other *12 Codes of Evolution,* is imperative to the survival of our species.

The New Human is a term gaining popularity as the concepts of Conscious Evolution and the Shift become mainstream. It is generally agreed upon among futurists, philosophers, metaphysicians, scientists, and the world's indigenous leaders (both contemporary and ancient) that the New Human will have increased strands (up to 12) of DNA. The increase of DNA strands occurs with a process called activation. Activations are already occurring individually and en masse, through conscious deliberation or unconscious psychic phenomena known as downloading. This activation process affects genetic, molecular, and glandular changes, allowing higher frequencies of energetic or divine vibration to govern the individual's body, mind, and spirit. DNA activation connects the individual with their energetic layers and universal layers of consciousness. The new human will have superior telekinetic and telepathic capabilities, making miracles and serendipity commonplace. This ideology differs from Transhumanism in that new human enhancements occur through consciousness-raising rather than technological advances.

The New Humanity of Homo sapiens (wise man) will be telepathically connected to each other, the Earth, and the universe through the Noosphere. Humans will be fully cooperative with each other and with energetic or divine principles, existing harmoniously with nature and the universe. Democratic and altruistic principles will govern all aspects of human endeavor. There is a growing body of speculation that Homo sapiens already exist as differing species. Frank White, author of *The Overview Effect: Space Exploration and Human Evolution* (1998), told Barbara Marx Hubbard in August 2012 during a Maestro phone conference that he believes we should start calling ourselves Homo egoicus (rather than Homo sapiens) because we are entrenched in our egoic minds. He posits we can then begin to differentiate, for example, by calling ourselves Homo transitionalis, while we collectively work toward becoming Homo holisticus or Homo luminous. White further believes a new genus is evolving. He is naming it Psyche Materialis (soul in the material) and believes that the individuals of this genus of humankind will have fully-functioning Christ-like, Homo-luminous light-bodies.

Tricksters are ancient, archetypal figures found in mythologies worldwide. They appear as animals, humans, spirits, or gods who disrupt order, bend the rules, and reveal hidden truths through chaos, mischief, or inversion. In traditional stories, they are agents of transformation, challenging norms and catalyzing unexpected growth. Coyote in Native American lore, Loki in Norse mythology, and Anansi in West African stories are classic examples. In contemporary New Age discourse, the term *trickster* has taken on a more cautionary meaning. It is increasingly used to describe supernatural or interdimensional entities that pose as light beings or ascended guides but carry deceptive or self-serving intentions. These entities may lure seekers through flattery, false promises, or energetic mimicry. They encourage channeling, dependency, or, in extreme cases, energetic possession. In CP, tricksters are considered part of the broader consciousness ecosystem. They do not necessarily represent "evil" but rather unintegrated shadows within the psyche and the cosmos. Their presence calls for discernment, boundary-setting, and inner alignment. They may appear when the ego seeks shortcuts, trauma seeks relief, or the seeker is making progress on their spiritual path, for example, when they are ready to transcend illusion.

- **Ultimate healing** is not observable, although its results can be identified in states of peace and knowing that nothing is more critical than BEing.
- **Ultra-terrestrials** are beings of the highest order who are, according to Hurtak, directly connected to the divine source, God, or the Christ consciousness.
- **Vibration** is the rhythmic movement of energy at the most fundamental level of being. In CP, vibration reflects the state of one's consciousness in motion, how thoughts, emotions, intentions, and life force oscillate within and around the body. Every being has a vibrational signature, an invisible song, which can shift, distort, or harmonize depending on coherence, awareness, and alignment. It is a living waveform, the pulse of our presence, and it indicates where we are in our state of becoming.
- **Walk-in** is a concept dating back to Hindu literature, in which one's soul has been merged with that of another, typically considered to be a higher being, such as an angel or an ultra-terrestrial entity. However, many tricksters are less evolved beings who masquerade as benevolent entities. They can include extraterrestrial beings. (See ultra-terrestrial beings, tricksters, and discernment.)
- **Woke** began as a metaphysical concept in the 19th century, urging humanity to awaken from the sleep of ignorance. Teachers like G.I. Gurdjieff and Maurice Nicoll spoke of the human tendency to live in a state of psychic sleep—mechanical, unaware, and vulnerable to manipulation due to spiritual degeneration. Manly P. Hall warned that without conscious awakening, humanity drifts into degenerative states of being. The term later emerged in African American Vernacular English (AAVE) as a call to vigilance, activism, and awareness of racism, oppression, and social inequity—a powerful signal of social and moral awakening. In recent years, however, *woke* has been **co-opted and weaponized** by reactionary movements seeking to dismiss or distort progressive ideals. What once signified *care for the soul and justice for the oppressed* has become a cultural flashpoint, dividing communities and conflating consciousness teachings with identity politics. It stands as a prime example of the hijacking of sacred language. In Celestial Psychology®, we recognize *woke* as both a cultural and spiritual signal—one that must be reclaimed and anchored as a genuine call to justice, discernment, and awakening.
- **Zero Point** is an altered state of consciousness, often associated with deep meditation, hypnosis, or spontaneous mystical experience. It is frequently equated with the Alpha or even Theta brainwave states, where one is simultaneously alert yet aware of profound stillness. It is also known as a field of nothingness that paradoxically feels full and profoundly rich at the same time. Many experience a sense of unity, timelessness, or direct communion with Source.
- **Zero Point Energy (ZPE)** and **Zero Fluctuation Field (ZFF)** are terms rooted in quantum physics, first explored by Albert Einstein and Otto Stern in 1913.

Glossary

Initially, it was thought that a vacuum existed between sub-atomic particles in every atom. But as quantum science evolved, it was discovered that what appeared to be "empty space" is actually seething with activity—particles and waves flickering into and out of existence at the quantum level. This so-called "vacuum" is now recognized as a quantum field of infinite potential—a sea of pure possibilities from which energy and matter spontaneously arise. This is the *Zero Point*, the origin point of creation, where form emerges from formlessness. ZPE and ZFF describe this field of subtle energy that underlies all existence, operating as a divine blueprint for matter, energy, and consciousness. In metaphysical terms, Zero Point is not only a concept in physics but a doorway to spiritual remembrance—an inner space of stillness where the ego dissolves and one encounters the pulse of the cosmos.

BIBLIOGRAPHY & SUGGESTED READING

Arguellis, Jose. *Manifesto for the Noosphere: The Next Stage in the Evolution of Human Consciousness.* Berkley, CA: Evolver Editions/North Atlantic Books, 2011.

Barsotti, Tiffany, J. *The Biology of Transformation: The Physiology of Presence and Spiritual Transcendence.* Lulu Publishing Services, 2022.

Beres, Derek & Remski, Matthew & Walker, Julian. *Conspirituality: How New Age Conspiracy Theories Became a Health Threat.* NY: Hatchett Book Group, 2023.

Blesdoe, Chris. *UFO of God: The Extraordinary True Story of Chris Bledsoe.* 2023.

Bletzer, June G. *The Encyclopedic Psychic Dictionary.* Lithia Springs, GA: New Leaf Distributing Co., 1986.

Braden, Gregg. *The Divine Matrix: Bridging Time, Space, Miracles and Belief.* Carlsbad, CA: Hay House, 2007.

—. The Science of Self-Empowerment: Awakening the New Human Story. Carlsbad, CA: Hay House, 2017.

Brennan, Barbara Ann. *Hands of Light: A Guide to Healing Through the Human Energy Field.* New York, NY: Bantam, 1987

Cohen, Andrew. *Evolutionary Enlightenment: A New Path to Spiritual Awakening.* New York, NY: Select Books, 2011.

Cotton, Michael. *Source Code Meditation: Hacking Evolution through Higher Brain Activation.* Rochester, Vermont: Findhorn Press, 2018.

de Chardin, Teilhard. *The Divine Milieu.* New York, NY: Harper & Row, 1960.

—. *The Future of Man.* New York, NY: Harper & Row, 1964.

Dooley, Mike. *The Great Awakening: Our Prophesied Transformation and the Attainment of Embodied Enlightenment.* Orlando, FL: TUT Enterprises, 2024.

Dowd, Michael. *Thank God for Evolution: How the Marriage of Science and Religion Will Transform Your Life and Our World.* New York: Plume Press, 2009.

Bibliography & Suggested Reading

Dyer, Wayne. *There is a Spiritual Solution to Every Problem.* New York: Quill Publishers, 2003.

Gallo, Fred & Vincenzi, Harry. *Energy Tapping.* Oakland, CA: New Harbinger Publications, 2008.

Goswami, Amit. *The Self-Aware Universe—How Consciousness Creates the Material World.* New York, NY: Penguin Putnam, 1993.

Hall, Judy. *The Encyclopedia of Crystals.* Beverly, MA: Quayside Publishing Group, 2006.

Hall, Manly P. *The Secret Teachings of All Times.* New York, NY: Penguin, 2003

Harvey, Andrew. *The Hope: A Guide to Sacred Activism.* New York: Hay House, 2009.

Hubbard, Barbara Marx. *52 Codes for Conscious Evolution.* Santa Barbara, CA: Foundation for Conscious Evolution, 2011.

—. *Birth 2012 and Beyond: Humanity's Great Shift to the Age of Conscious Evolution.* Shift Books, 2012.

—. *Conscious Evolution: Awaking the Power of Our Social Potential.* Novato, CA: New World Library, 1998.

—. *Emergence: The Shift from Ego to Essence: Ten Steps to the Universal Human.* Charlottesville, VA: Hampton Roads Publishing, 2001.

—. *The Evolutionary Journey: A Personal Guide To A Positive Future.* San Francisco, CA: Evolutionary Press, 1982.

Hurtak, Desiree, and James J. Hurtak. *The Overself Awakening: A Guide for the Schoolhouse of the Soul: Transitions Through Our Consciousness Time Zone.* Los Gatos, CA: The Academy for Future Science, 2011.

Hurtak, James J. *The Book of Knowledge—The Keys of Enoch.* Los Gatos, CA: The Academy for Future Science, 1977.

Johnson, Kurt, and David Robert Ord. *The Coming Interspiritual Age.* Vancouver: Namaste, 2012.

Laszlow, Ervin. *Reconnecting to the Source: The New Science of Spiritual Experience, How It Can Change You, and How It Can Transform the World*. New York, St Martins Press, 2020.

Lipton, Bruce. *The Biology of Belief: Unleashing the Power of Consciousness, Matter and Miracles*. Carlsbad, CA: Hay House, 2005.

Losey, Meg Blackburn. *The Secret History of Consciousness*. San Francisco, CA: Weiser Books, 2010.

—. *Touching the Light: What Miracles Are Made Of*. San Francisco, CA: Weiser Books, 2011.

Magana, Sergio. *2012-2021:The Dawn of the Sixth Sun: The Path of Quetzalcoatl*. Edited, Endorsement by Irvin Laszlo. Torino: Blooming Books, 2012.

Mattingly, Celeste. *Celestial Psychology: A Workbook for Chakras, Psychological Theory & Conscious Evolution*. Adam Kadmon Publishing, West Hartford, CT. 2013

Mattingly, Celeste. *Celestial Psychology: A Guidebook for Creating Miracles, Luminosity & Conscious Evolution*. Adam Kadmon Publishing, West Hartford, CT. Original 2013, Revised 2019.

McTaggart, Lynne. *The Field: The Quest for the Secret Force of the Universe*. New York, NY: Harper Collins Publishers, 2008.

Mollon, Phil. *Blue Diamond Healing*. UK: Ashford Colour Press, 2022

Philosophy Now: a magazine of ideas. Issue 166. London, 2025.

Phipps, Carter. *Evolutionaries: Unlocking the Spiritual and Cultural Potential of Science's Greatest Idea*. New York: Harper Perennial, 2012.

Pierrakos, Eva. *The Pathwork of Self-Transformation*. New York, NY: Bantam Books, 1990.

Pierrakos, John. *Core Energetics: Developing the Capacity to Love and Heal*. Mendocino, CA: Liferhythms, 1990.

"Pierre Teilhard de Chardin (Letters to Mme Georges-Marie Haardt)." n.d.

Silva, Freddie. *The Divine Blueprint: Temples, Power Places, and the Global Plan to Shape the Human Soul*. 2012

Bibliography & Suggested Reading

Steinfeld, Alan. *Making Contact: Preparing for the New Realities of Extraterrestrial Existence.* New York: St. Martin's Press, 2021.

The Holomovement: Embracing our Collective Purpose to Unite Humanity. Edited by Kuntzelman & Robinson, Light on Light Press: Fort Lauderdale, FL, 2023.

Jones, Joness, and Thompson, Eric W. *A Subtle Energy Field Guide: An Ocean in a Drop.* Joness Jones Studio, 2022.

Tolle, Eckhart. *A New Earth– Awakening to Your Life's Purpose.* New York: Plume Publishing, 2005.

Twyman, James F. *I Don't Know, Maybe, I Love You: How to De-Polarize Your Family, Business, Country, and the World.* Intervale, NH: Summit Press, 2025.

Vergera, Miguel Angel. *The Sacred Knowledge of the Maya: The Spiritual Message of the Maya Symbols in their Temples and Pyramids.* 2011.

—, and Trudy Woodcock. *Maya Goddesses: The Return of the Maya Priestesses.* 2022.

Villoldo, Alberto. *The Four Insights: Wisdom, Power, and Grace of the Earthkeepers.* Carlsbad, CA: Hay House, 2006.

White, Frank. *The Overview Effect: Space Exploration and Human Evolution.* 1998

Williamson, Marianne. *The Law of Divine Compensation: On Work, Money, and Miracles.* New York, NY: Harper Collins Publishers, 2012.

ABOUT THE AUTHOR

Celeste Emelia Mattingly, LCSW, is a pioneering psychotherapist, teacher, and visionary creator of *Celestial Psychology*®. This transformational framework integrates psychology, metaphysics, energy medicine, and quantum healing into a unified path of evolutionary consciousness. Her work radiates with a rare fusion of fierce love and luminous wisdom. Celeste's writing, teaching, and healing practices invite others into a living experience of wholeness, empowering them to become conscious co-creators of their inner and outer worlds.

This book and its dedication, *"The Ascension of Humanity, Gaia, Mother Earth & the entire Cosmos!"* embody her life's mission: to help catalyze the global shift from survival to *thrival*, from fragmentation to coherence, from a fear-based existence to a loving, radiant BEcoming. Celeste offers her readers, students, and clients tools, ideas, and a sacred call to participate in the great evolutionary dance unfolding within and around us.

A graduate of the MSW Advanced Generalist Program at Springfield College in Springfield, MA, she has over forty years of experience working in various recovery settings. She founded Psychotherapy Healing Services, LLC in 1999, and in 2023, she incorporated Celestial Empowerment Quantum Healthcare, LLC to expand her work on a global level.

Celeste began her metaphysical studies in the 1970s. Her ongoing studies include *A Course in Miracles* and the Twelve Steps. In 2002, she completed Reiki Level I & II training in the USUI tradition. That year, she also became a minister in the Universal Life Church. In 2008, she became a facilitator of the Reconnective® healing method. She graduated from Barbara Marx Hubbard's *Ego to Essence* and the *Agents of Conscious Evolution* (ACE) trainings. From 2008 to 2023, she extensively studied alternative healing methods with Eugenius (Gene) Ang, PhD, a Yale-trained neurobiologist and energy healing practitioner from California. In June 2024, she became a certified practitioner of the 13th Octave LaHoChi healing modality. In April 2025, she completed the training to teach this upcoming and timely modality for Ascension.

About the Author

Celeste is one of the few practitioners offering Tachyon Healing and Anti-Aging Meditation Sessions at *Celestial Empowerment Quantum Healthcare*, Farmington, CT.

She also hosts workshops approved by the National Association of Social Workers (NASW) for professionals, as well as ongoing gatherings for meditation, healing, and spiritual empowerment for laypersons.

For more information, visit: https://celestialempowerment.com
Contact by email: cmattingly100@comcast.net

INDEX

13th Octave LaHoChi xxvi, xxvii, 94, 163, 164, 183, 195
5D 163, 164, 175
A Course in Miracles 195
activation 165, 187
acupuncture 165, 171, 179
altered states 120, 180
anthropomorphic 64, 92
Argüelles .... x, xviii, 121, 181
Ascended Masters 95, 163, 183
ascension 164, 187
Association for Comprehensive Energy Psychology (ACEP) 83, 172
aura (auric field) 32, 33, 164
Celestial Psychology
    ensures 165
chakra(s) 165
    Sanskrit 120
Chi 165, 176
co-create 167
conscious evolution 87, 167
consciousness
    altered 120, 189
    defined 167
    states of 180, 189
consciousness-raising 87, 118, 164, 167, 176, 182
conspiracy theories 139, 143, 146, 168, 177
conspirituality 148, 168
Dark Enlightenment xxvii, 144, 169, 177
Darwin, Charles 173
de Chardin, Pierre Teilhard 121
dimensions xi, xiii, xv, xxvi, 51, 55, 69, 79, 95, 124, 125, 130, 147, 163, 169, 170, 179, 183, 185, 186, 187
discernment 49, 51, 68, 81, 82, 84, 139, 143, 145, 148, 149, 150, 151, 168, 169, 177, 182, 183, 184, 188, 189

Divine Feminine .... xxiv, 164, 170
DNA 32
DNA activation 170, 188
dogma .... xix, 117, 173
Earthkeepers 32
effector (action) 92
electromagnetic energy 164, 171
Emotional Freedom Technique (EFT) 172, 179
energy medicine 171, 172
enlightenment .. 117, 119, 120, 134, 135
Enlightenment Era 117
epigenetics 64, 172
essence 120, 134, 173, 182, 185
etheric 32
evolutionary
    energy 119
    enlightenment 120
    kaleidoscope 64, 174
    trajectory 174, 175
evolutionary codes x
free will 159, 178
frequency xiv, xviii, xx, xxi, 38, 40, 43, 49, 50, 51, 53, 54, 65, 68, 70, 76, 83, 93, 95, 128, 130, 131, 143, 163, 166, 171, 173, 175, 178, 180, 183, 184, 187
genus 186, 188
God 167, 185, 189
Great Shift 187
Harvey 147, 192
healing 119, 167, 195
    divine 185
    pranic 172
    relative 184
    Shamanism 172
    spiritual 32
    ultimate 189
Higher Power 167

Higher Self 181
hijacking 139
Holy Work 176, 182
Homo
  holisticus 188
  luminous 32, 186, 188
  sapiens 32, 63, 188
  transitionalis 188
  universalis 186
Homo angelicus 76, 186
Homo egoicus 76, 188
Hopi 32
Hubbard, Barbara Marx 185, 188
Human Energy System (HES) 171, 176
Hunab Kuix, x, xi, xii, xiii, xiv, xv, xix, xxii, 97, 99, 101, 103, 105, 107, 109, 111
Hunab Ku, the Mayan Galactic Butterfly ix
Hurtak, James J. (JJ) 189
Hybrids 79, 80, 177
hypnosis 181, 189
imaginal cells 177
Inca (Inka) 32
infodemic 145, 177
Integral Membrane Proteins (IMPs) 92
interspirituality 178
intuition 180
Jesus Christ 171, 187, 188, 189
Jose Argüelles x
Jung, Carl Gustav 166, 185
Kālī 147, 178
Kant, Immanuel 117, 118
karma 163
Kirlian photography 33, 164
Lady Zak Kuuk xxiv
Light Language 46, 178
lightworkers .... xviii, xx
Lightworkers37, 43, 88, 141, 144, 153, 177
Lipton, Bruce 64, 92
lulz 142, 179
luminosity 32, 33, 164, 170, 174
Luminous Energy Field (LEF) 171
Maya (Mayan) 32, 187
medical intuitive 165
meliorism 35, 37, 159

meridian (meridian point)165, 177, 179
merkabah 179
metamorphosis 117, 177
Metaphysicians 37, 170
metaphysics 92, 172, 179
Miguel Angel Vergara xxiv
miracle 162
miracles59, 65, 76, 77, 108, 159, 162, 188
New Age 117
New Thought (New Thought Movement) 64, 65
noosphere 42, 120, 175, 188
oneness 115, 118, 187
photobiomodulation (PBM) 127
Pranic Healing® 181
pronoia ....xxiii, 159, 182
psyche 166
Psyche Materialis 188
Quality of Life 69, 118
Quantity of Light 69, 182
quantum leap 32, 69
quantum physics 33
quantum theory 183
receptor (awareness) 92
reciprocal nourishment 56, 171
recovery .... iv, 54, 195
spirit 161
spiritual 65, 69, 115, 118, 119
spirituality 172, 174
*Starseeds*37, 43, 79, 80, 88, 141, 171, 177, 186
stem cells 74, 127, 128
supraconscious creators 186
tachyon .... xiii, 124, 125, 128, 129
Tachyon 131
telepathic 120
theology 32
transformation 173, 180
Tricksters 81, 188
Trudy Woodcock .... xxiv, 194
unconscious 166, 167
  collective 166
Vernadsky, Vladimir 121
Villoldo, Alberto 32, 176
visionaries 187
wake up 162

White, Frank 188
Wilber, Ken 119
Williamson 146, 194
woke 142, 189

Women's Liberation Movement 167
zero point 189
zero point energy (ZPE) 189

ENDNOTES

[i] (Villoldo 2006, ix) Laika are the Andean and Amazonian "Earthkeepers." They are the guardians of sacred medicine wisdom thought to have been lost at the time of the Spanish Conquest of South America. They came out of seclusion from high in the Andes in 1950 "to offer all the people the wisdom that would sustain us through the great changes we were about to face, which would help us alter our reality and give birth to a better world."

[ii] (Villoldo 2006, xiii)

[iii] EMP Mattingly, 2012

[iv] Hall 2003, 261

[v] (Cosmides 1997)

[vi] (Lipton 2005, 52)

[vii] Lipton says, "The notion of cells as miniature humans ... would be considered heresy by most biologists. Trying to explain the nature of anything not human by relating it to human behavior is called anthropomorphism." (Lipton 2005, 5)

[viii] Hall 2003, 39, 270

[ix] (website Sahtouris)

[x] (Hubbard, The Evolutionary Journey: A Personal Guide To A Positive Future 1982, 35)

[xi] (Lipton 2005, 56)

[xii] (Johnson and Ord 2012, 9)

[xiii] (Perlmutter and Villoldo 2011, xxiii)

[xiv] (Cohen 2011, 27)

[xv] (de Chardin 1964, 163)

[xvi] (Cohen 2011, 27)

[xvii] (Perlmutter and Villoldo 2011, xxv–xxvii)

[xviii] (Tolle 2005, 123)

www.ingramcontent.com/pod-product-compliance
Lightning Source LLC
Chambersburg PA
CBHW070634100426
42744CB00006B/675